Are You Making the Most of Your Money?
A Personal Guide for Achieving Financial Success

Are You Making the Most of Your Money? A Personal Guide for Achieving Financial Success

By Christopher Truman Pierce

ISBN-13: 978-0-6457036-1-0

I dedicate this book to my beautiful wife, Faye, who has always supported me and believed in my dreams. Your love and encouragement have been my rock through the ups and downs of life, and I am grateful to have you by my side.

I also dedicate this book to my son and daughter, Alex and Diane. Watching you grow and learn has been one of the greatest joys of my life. I hope that the lessons and principles contained within these pages will help you to achieve financial success and happiness in your own lives.

Thank you to my family for your love and support. I could not have achieved any level of financial success without you.

With love and gratitude,
Chris

Contents

Preface

Are you making the most of your money? If you're like most people, you may be unsure of the answer to this question. Managing your finances can be a daunting and confusing task, especially if you're not sure where to start. That's where this book comes in.

In "Are You Making the Most of Your Money? A Personal Guide for Achieving Financial Success," Christopher Truman Pierce, a veteran of the financial services industry, provides a comprehensive overview of the key concepts and strategies that you need to know to take control of your financial situation and achieve your goals.

Whether you're looking to save for retirement, pay off debt, or simply improve your financial literacy, this book has something for you. From setting financial goals and creating a budget, to saving regularly and investing wisely, you'll find the guidance and tools you need to succeed.

In addition to the main content of the book, you'll also find chapters on credit and debt management, building a diversified income stream, tax planning and preparation, and protecting your finances. Whether you're just starting out on your financial journey or are well on your way to success, this book has something to offer.

If you're ready to take control of your money and start making the most of your financial resources, then this book is for you. Let Christopher Truman Pierce be your guide on this exciting journey towards financial success.

Making the Most of Your Money

I had been working as a financial analyst at a major national savings and loan bank for the past two years. I was based at the corporate level, and my desk was on the same floor as the CEO and CFO of the company. While I had always been interested in finance, I must admit that I was starting to get a little bored with my job. Things got even more complicated when I got involved in a failed office romance with a co-worker. Although we tried to keep things secret, it was impossible to completely hide our relationship from our colleagues. As a result, I found myself having to work with my ex-girlfriend on a daily basis, which was awkward to say the least.

My boss was a hard-charging executive in charge of financial forecasting for the bank. He was a demanding boss and expected his tasks to be completed quickly and efficiently. However, I often found myself under pressure to complete other assignments that were of less interest to him, which made it difficult for me to keep up with his demands.

Just before I was planning to go on a long-planned vacation, my boss called me into his office and informed me that I was being placed in a performance management program. This is a precursor to being fired, and I knew that my boss had a reputation for letting go of employees who didn't meet his expectations. I was shocked and overwhelmed by this news. I had always been a diligent worker, but I guess it wasn't enough to impress my boss. I was also overcome with fear about my financial situation. I had been planning to attend graduate school in about nine months, but I wasn't sure how I was going to support myself until then.

In that moment, I made the impulsive decision to quit on the spot. I knew that I didn't want to work for a boss who wasn't happy with my performance, and I also knew that I needed to focus on my own goals and plans.

Looking back on that experience, I can see how having financial security is so important. It gave me the freedom to make a difficult decision and pursue my dreams, even when things didn't go as planned. It's a lesson that I carry with me to this day.

Taking back control

When financial meltdown struck, I realized that I needed to take control of my financial future. Determined to turn things around, I started making changes. Tracking spending and setting up a budget were the first steps. After starting graduate school, I learned about investing and started putting a little money into the stock market each month. My goal was to get out of debt and become financially stable.

At first, staying on track was difficult and required many sacrifices. Frustration and overwhelm set in as it seemed like I was taking one step forward and two steps back. But I stayed focused, and progress soon followed. Paying off debt and building up savings brought a sense of pride and accomplishment. I had taken control of my financial future and felt more secure.

My recovery from financial hardship was not easy, but it was worth it. Learning to be more mindful and responsible with my money has made all the difference. Now, I live a more comfortable life with everything I need. Most importantly, I rest easy at night knowing that my financial future is secure. I want you to be able to say the same, and I think this book can help.

Understand the importance of managing your money

Managing your money is important because it can help you to achieve your financial goals, such as saving for retirement or buying a house. It can also help you to avoid financial stress and difficulties, such as being unable to pay your bills or being in debt. By taking control of your finances and making smart decisions about how to spend and save your money, you can improve your financial well-being and set yourself up for a more secure financial future.

Everyone's financial situation and goals are different, but some general advice for achieving financial freedom and security include:

1. Establish financial goals: What are you trying to accomplish with improvements to your finances? Spelling-out your goals is critical to achieving financial success.
2. Create a budget and stick to it: This will help you track your income and expenses and identify areas where you can cut back or save more.
3. Save regularly and invest wisely: Building an emergency fund and investing in a diverse range of assets can help protect your financial security in the long run.
4. Credit and Debt Management: High-interest debt, such as credit card debt, can be a major drain on your finances. Prioritizing its repayment can free up more money to save and invest.
5. Build a diversified income stream: Depending on a single source of income can be risky. Consider ways to diversify your income, such as starting a side hustle or investing in passive income streams.
6. Tax Planning and Preparation: Managing your taxes to minimize your liabilities and maximize your deductions and credits.
7. Protecting your Finances: Safeguarding your assets and income from unexpected events and losses.

These topic areas constitute an outline for the rest of the book, although they are also summarized in short form within this chapter below. It is important to read the details in each chapter, however, since not all advise applies equally to everyone. As the saying goes, 'The devil is in the details,' and this holds particularly true for personal finances. In addition, general advice is easier to understand when explained in the context of the financial situations that you face.

Establish financial goals

When I was in my late twenties, I felt like I was stuck in a rut. I was working long hours and struggling to make ends meet. I was starting to feel like my finances were controlling me instead of the other way around. That is, when I decided to take a step back and re-evaluate my goals. I started to think about what was truly important to me and what I wanted to accomplish. I soon realized that I wanted to be able to pursue my passions and have the financial freedom to do things that made me happy.

I created a plan to get there. I set up a budget and started tracking my spending. I began to save a little each month and put it towards my goals. I also started to invest in myself, taking classes and learning new skills that would help me reach my goals. It took a lot of hard work and dedication, but I eventually achieved my goal of financial freedom. Now, I'm able to pursue my passions and live a life that's true to my values. It feels amazing to be in control of my finances and to be living the life that I want.

My experience demonstrates that, while having more money can be a goal for some people, it is not the only financial goal that people have. Some other common financial goals include:

- Buying a home: Achieving the dream of homeownership by saving for a down payment and securing a mortgage.
- Funding a child's education: Investing in a child's future success by saving for college or other education expenses.
- Planning for retirement: Securing a comfortable future after work by saving and investing for retirement.
- Saving for a major purchase, such as a car or vacation: Preparing for a significant expenditure by setting aside money over time.
- Becoming financially independent: Achieving financial freedom and self-sufficiency by building wealth and reducing reliance on external sources of income.
- Giving back: For some people, giving back to their community or supporting a cause they care about is an important financial goal. This might involve donating money to charity or volunteering their time and skills.

Choosing among financial goals is often related to a person's values and priorities. Different people have different values and priorities, and these can influence their financial goals. For example, someone who values security and stability might prioritize building an emergency fund, while someone who values giving back to their community might prioritize donating to charity. It is important to consider your values and priorities when setting financial goals, as this can help ensure that your goals, once achieved, align with what is most important to you.

Consider what is most important to you. It's easy to say "more money," but for what purpose? Be honest about your goals with respect to your financial future so that you can accurately assess progress. Keep in mind that once you reach your goals (and I believe you will), you can revise your expectations and find new goals to pursue. Take some time to deeply think about what truly matters to you.

Establishing clear financial goals is related to creating a budget because they both involve setting priorities and making decisions about how to allocate your money. By setting financial goals, you can identify what is most important to you and determine how much money you need to achieve your goals. This can help you create a budget that aligns with your values and priorities and motivate you to stick to your budget to achieve your goals. By setting financial goals and creating an aligned budget, you can take control of your financial situation and make progress towards achieving your objectives.

Create a budget and stick to it

Creating and sticking to a personal budget is an important step towards achieving financial stability. To create a budget, start by tracking your spending for a few weeks to get an idea of where your money is going. Then, identify your fixed expenses, such as rent or mortgage payments and utility bills, as well as your variable expenses, such as groceries and entertainment. Next, set a budget for each category and determine how much money you have left over for savings and debt repayment. It's important to regularly review your budget and adjust as needed. To stick to your budget, try setting up automatic payments for fixed expenses and using cash or debit for variable expenses. It can also be helpful to set financial goals and rewards to motivate yourself to stay on track. Once you have identified your financial goals and created a budget, it's important to take the next step and start saving regularly and investing wisely.

Save regularly and invest wisely

Saving regularly and investing wisely are key to building financial security and wealth. To save regularly, start by setting a savings goal and determining how much you can afford to save each month. Then, automate your savings by setting up a direct deposit from your paycheck or a regular transfer from your checking account to your savings account. It's also important to avoid impulse purchases and resist the temptation to dip into your savings unless it's for a true emergency.

To invest wisely, start by educating yourself about the different types of investments and their associated risks. Then, consider your goals, time horizon, and risk tolerance to determine an appropriate investment mix. It's also important to diversify your investments and regularly review and rebalance your portfolio to ensure that it continues to align with your goals and risk tolerance. Finally, be mindful of fees and avoid making emotional decisions about your investments. Working with a financial advisor can be helpful if you're unsure about how to invest wisely. Final decisions, however, must always be made by you. Only you have the incentives to make investments that are in your best interests.

Credit and debt management are related to proper investment decisions because they can impact your financial situation and ability to invest. Good credit and manageable debt can give you access to low-interest loans and credit, which can help you finance investments and grow your wealth. On the other hand, bad credit and excessive debt can limit your borrowing power and increase the cost of borrowing, which can make it more difficult to invest and achieve your financial goals. By managing your credit and debt effectively, you can improve your financial situation and make more informed investment decisions.

Credit and debt management

High-interest debt can be a financial burden and it's important to pay it off as soon as possible. To pay off high-interest debt, start by creating a budget and identifying any excess income that can be applied towards your debt. Consider consolidating your debt to take advantage of lower interest rates, if possible. Then, create a plan to pay off your debt using the debt snowball or debt avalanche method. The debt snowball method involves paying off your smallest debts first, while the debt avalanche method involves paying off your debts with the highest interest rates first.

It's also important to avoid accumulating new debt while you're paying off your existing debt. This may mean making sacrifices and cutting back on discretionary spending. It's also important to be disciplined and stick to your plan. It may take time to pay off your debt, but the sense of accomplishment and financial freedom that comes with being debt-free can be well worth the effort.

Once you have taken steps to manage your credit and debt, it's important to consider the next steps in your financial journey, such as building a diversified income stream to increase your financial stability and security.

Build a diversified income stream

To build a diversified income stream, it's important to have multiple sources of income that provide you with a steady flow of money. This can help you reduce financial risk and increase your financial stability. To create a diversified income stream, start by identifying your skills, interests, and goals, and then explore different types of income sources, such as part-time or freelance work, rental income, or investments. It's also important to balance potential return with risk, and to maintain flexibility and adaptability in order to respond to changes in your financial situation. Regularly review and adjust your income stream to ensure that it continues to align with your goals and needs. By building a diversified income stream, you can take control of your financial future and achieve financial stability and security. Once you have built a diversified income stream, it's important to consider the tax implications and take steps to plan and prepare your taxes effectively.

Tax planning and preparation

Tax planning and preparation are important aspects of managing your finances and maximizing your wealth. To effectively plan and prepare your taxes, start by staying informed about the latest tax laws and changes. Then, track your income and expenses throughout the year, and take advantage of tax-saving opportunities, such as contributing to a retirement account or claiming eligible deductions and credits. It's also important to accurately report your income and claim all your eligible deductions and credits, and to seek help from a tax professional if you're unsure about how to handle your taxes. By planning and preparing your taxes carefully, you can minimize your liabilities and maximize your tax savings, and help ensure that you're in compliance with the law. Once you have completed your tax planning and preparation, it's important to consider the next steps in managing your finances, such as protecting your assets and income.

Protect your finances

To protect your finances, it's important to take steps to safeguard your assets and income from unexpected events and losses. This can help you maintain financial stability and security, and ensure that you're able to weather financial challenges and setbacks. To protect your finances, start by assessing your current financial situation and identifying potential risks, such as job loss or unexpected expenses. Then, take steps to mitigate these risks, such as by building an emergency fund, purchasing insurance, or creating a backup plan. It's also important to regularly review and update your financial plan and protection measures, and to seek help from a financial advisor if you're unsure about how to best protect your finances. By taking steps to protect your finances, you can reduce your financial risk and increase your financial security.

The next steps towards financial success

Congratulations on taking the first step towards financial success by reading this introduction and overview. Whether you're looking to improve your financial situation, pay off debt, save for a major purchase, or build wealth, the information and strategies in this book can help you achieve your goals.

You may be feeling overwhelmed or unsure of where to start, but know that you are not alone. Millions of people struggle with their finances, but with the right knowledge and support, anyone can learn to manage their money effectively and achieve financial stability and security. As you continue to explore the pages of this book, you will learn practical and proven techniques for budgeting, saving, investing, and more. You will also gain valuable insights and inspiration from the stories of people who have overcome financial challenges and achieved their goals. With dedication and commitment, you can succeed on your financial journey. Take the next step and continue reading to discover the tools and strategies you need to achieve your financial goals. You can achieve financial success, and this book can help you get there.

Establishing Financial Goals

As a financial analyst with a degree in economics, I was trained to think about money in a certain way. But sometimes, life has a way of interrupting our preconceived notions. That's what happened to me when I bounced a check drawn on my own bank. It was a wakeup call that made me realize I had gotten a little careless with my spending. Suddenly, I was in a financial bind and I knew I needed to do something about it.

To make matters worse, my boss confronted me about the bounced check, and I knew I had to act. At first, I was tempted to just throw in the towel and go back to my old habits of living paycheck to paycheck. But then I realized that if I didn't get a handle on my finances, I was never going to be able to achieve my financial goals.

It was a turning point for me. I realized that I needed to shift my perspective on personal finance and start viewing it as something more than just a boring subject. With a little bit of discipline and planning, I was able to get a handle on my money and achieve my financial dreams.

This experience taught me that sometimes, it takes a crisis to make us re-evaluate our priorities and shift our perspective. If you're struggling with understanding your financial goals or just find personal finance to be a drag, don't give up. With the right mindset and a commitment to improving your financial situation, you can succeed.

The importance of setting financial goals

It's important to set financial goals in the context of understanding your values and priorities because your values and priorities will determine what you want to achieve with your money, and how you prioritize spending and saving. By understanding your values and priorities, you can set financial goals that align with what is most important to you, and that motivate and inspire you to take action. This can help you create a budget that reflects your values and priorities, and make decisions about how to allocate your money in a way that aligns with your goals. By setting financial goals that reflect your values and priorities, you can make progress towards achieving what is most important to you and feel more satisfied and fulfilled with your financial situation.

Identifying your values and priorities

To identify your values and priorities, start by taking some time to reflect on what is most important to you in life. Think about what you value most, such as your family, health, career, or community. Consider what makes you happy and fulfilled, and what your goals and dreams are. Also, think about what you value in terms of your money and financial situation, such as security, independence, or generosity. Once you have a sense of what your values and priorities are, you can use this information to set financial goals that align with what is most important to you. You can also use your values and priorities to guide your decision-making and budgeting, and to evaluate whether your financial situation is meeting your needs and aligning with your goals.

Setting short-term, medium-term, and long-term goals

Short-term financial goals are goals that you want to achieve within the next year or so, such as paying off a credit card or building an emergency fund. Medium-term financial goals are goals that you want to achieve within the next five to ten years, such as saving for a down payment on a house or paying off student loans. Long-term financial goals are goals that you want to achieve over a longer period of time, such as saving for retirement or leaving an inheritance. To identify your short-term, medium-term, and long-term financial goals, start by thinking about what is most important to you and what you want to achieve in the short term, medium term, and long term. Then, consider your current financial situation and what you need to do in order to achieve your goals. You can also seek guidance from a financial advisor or planner to help you identify and prioritize your financial goals.

Evaluating your current financial situation

To evaluate your current financial situation, start by assessing your income, expenses, assets, and liabilities. This will give you a sense of how much money you have coming in and going out, and what you own and owe. You can use this information to calculate your net worth, which is the difference between your assets and liabilities. This will give you a snapshot of your financial situation and help you identify areas where you may need to make changes or improvements. You can also consider other factors, such as your credit score, debt-to-income ratio, and savings rate, which can impact your financial health and ability to achieve your goals. By evaluating your current financial situation, you can gain a better understanding of where you are now and what may be possible in the future.

Cash flow statement

Cash flow refers to the movement of money into and out of your personal finances. It is the difference between your income and your expenses, and it determines whether you have a surplus or deficit of cash. Income is the money that you receive from sources such as your salary, investments, or business profits. Expenses are the money that you spend on things such as housing, food, transportation, and entertainment. For example, if you earn $50,000 per year and spend $40,000 on expenses, your cash flow is $10,000, which is the surplus of income over expenses. However, if you earn $50,000 per year and spend $60,000 on expenses, your cash flow is -$10,000, which is the deficit of expenses over income. Managing your cash flow is important because it determines whether you have the funds available to pay your bills, save for the future, and achieve your financial goals.

A cash flow statement shows the movement of money into and out of your personal finances over a period, such as a week, a month, or a year. By examining your cash flow on a regular basis, you can track your income, expenses, and net cash flow, and identify trends and potential problems. For example, if you review your cash flow on a weekly basis, you can see whether you have enough money to cover your expenses for the week and make any necessary adjustments. If you review your cash flow monthly, you can see whether you have enough money to cover your expenses for the month and save for the future. If you review your cash flow on a yearly basis, you can see whether you have achieved your financial goals and make any necessary adjustments to your budget and financial plan. In summary, examining your cash flow on a regular basis can help you manage your money effectively and achieve your financial goals.

SAMPLE CASH FLOW STATEMENT

INCOME FOR JANUARY

Salary:	$3,500
Investment Income:	200
Total Income:	$3,700

EXPENSES

Rent:	$1,000
Food:	400
Utilities:	150
Transportation:	300
Entertainment:	100
Total Expenses:	$1,950
NET CASH FLOW:	$1,750

This cash flow statement shows that the individual had income of $3,700 from their salary and investments in the month of January. They also had expenses of $1,950 for rent, food, utilities, transportation, and entertainment. Their net cash flow was $1,750, which is the surplus of income over expenses. This surplus of cash indicates that the individual had sufficient funds to pay their bills and save for the future.

It is important to produce a personal cash flow statement because it can help you track your income, expenses, and net cash flow, and identify trends and potential problems. By examining your cash flow on a regular basis, you can make informed decisions about your financial activities and achieve your financial goals. For example, if you see that you are spending more money than you are earning, you can adjust your budget and expenses to improve your financial situation. If you see that you are not saving enough money for the future, you can increase your savings and investments to achieve your financial goals. In summary, a personal cash flow statement is an essential tool for managing your money effectively and achieving your financial goals. I encourage you to produce a personal cash flow statement now and review it on a regular basis to stay on track and achieve your financial goals.

Personal balance sheet

A personal balance sheet is a financial statement that shows a person's assets, liabilities, and net worth at a specific point in time. It is used to evaluate a person's financial health and can help them make informed decisions about their financial activities. The assets section of a personal balance sheet includes items that have value, such as cash, investments, real estate, and personal property. The liabilities section of a personal balance sheet includes items that represent a person's debts or financial obligations, such as credit card balances, mortgage or rent payments, student loans, and car loans. The net worth of a person is calculated by subtracting their liabilities from their assets. A positive net worth means that a person has more assets than liabilities, while a negative net worth means that a person has more liabilities than assets. In summary, a personal balance sheet is a financial statement that shows a person's assets, liabilities, and net worth at a specific point in time. It is used to evaluate a person's financial health and make informed decisions about their financial activities.

Here is a task list of how you can itemize your assets and liabilities to produce personal balance sheet:

1. Make a list of your assets, such as your cash, investments, real estate, vehicles, and personal property.
2. Include the value or estimated value of each asset, as well as any associated liabilities, such as mortgages or loans.

3. Be sure to include all your accounts, such as checking, savings, and investment accounts, as well as any physical assets, such as jewelry, valuable furniture, or collectibles.
4. Next, make a list of your liabilities, such as your debts, mortgages, and loans.
5. Include the balance or amount owed for each liability, as well as the interest rate and any minimum monthly payments.
6. Be sure to include all your debts, such as credit card balances, student loans, and car loans.

Typical assets that people have include cash, investments, real estate, vehicles, and personal property. More rare assets may include valuable collections, such as art or stamps, or business assets, such as patents or trademarks. Typical liabilities that people have include mortgages, loans, and credit card balances. More rare liabilities may include legal judgments (such as child support, spousal support), tax liens, or other obligations.

Here is an example of a typical list of assets and liabilities a person might have: Make up your own list based on what you own and what you owe to get a better picture of your present financial position.

SAMPLE PERSONAL BALANCE SHEET

ASSETS

Cash:	$1,000
Investments:	10,000
Real Estate:	250,000
Vehicles:	20,000
Personal Property:	5,000
Total Assets:	$286,000

LIABILITIES

Mortgage (@ 6.5% interest):	$150,000
Student Loan (@ 5 % interest):	30,000
Car Loan (@ 10% interest):	10,000
Credit Card (@ 21% interest):	5,000
Total Liabilities:	$195,000
NET WORTH:	$91,000

Banks often ask borrowers to produce a personal balance sheet because it is a financial statement that shows a person's assets, liabilities, and net worth at a specific point in time. This information is important for banks to evaluate the borrower's creditworthiness and determine their ability to repay a loan. A strong personal balance sheet can help insulate a borrower from stress related to poor cash flow, such as loss of a job, because it shows that they have assets that can be used to cover their expenses and liabilities in case of an emergency. For example, if a borrower has a positive net worth, it means that they have more assets than liabilities, which can provide them with a financial cushion in case of unexpected expenses or loss of income. On the other hand, if a borrower has a negative net worth, it means that they have more liabilities than assets, which can make them more vulnerable to financial stress and the risk of defaulting on their loan.

In summary, banks often ask borrowers to produce a personal balance sheet to evaluate their creditworthiness and determine their ability to repay a loan. A strong personal balance sheet can help insulate a borrower from stress related to poor cash flow, such as loss of a job, by showing that they have assets that can be used to cover their expenses and liabilities in case of an emergency. For instance, people can dip into savings or sell a car to help meet their loan payments.

Cash Flow is King!

Improvements to cash flow can ultimately benefit one's personal income statement because they can increase your net income or reduce your net loss. Cash flow is the movement of money into and out of your personal finances, while an income statement is a financial report that shows your net income or loss over a period of time. By improving your cash flow, you can increase your revenues and decrease your expenses, which can lead to a higher net income on your income statement. For example, if you increase your income through a higher paying job or additional income sources, and reduce your expenses through budgeting and cost-cutting, your net income on your income statement will increase. On the other hand, if you have a net loss on your income statement, improving your cash flow can help you reduce that loss and become profitable. In summary, improvements to cash flow can ultimately benefit a personal income statement by increasing your net income or reducing your net loss. For example, if you improve your cash flow by increasing your income and reducing your expenses, your net income on your income statement will increase, and if you have a net loss, improving your cash flow can help you reduce that loss and become profitable.

Financial trouble is always a consequence of problems with cash flow. If you have insufficient cash flow, you may not be able to meet your financial obligations, such as paying your bills, rent or mortgage, or credit card payments. As a result, you may fall behind on your payments and incur late fees, interest charges, or penalties. This can lead to financial distress and negatively impact your credit score, making it difficult to access credit or loans in the future. Furthermore, if you have insufficient cash flow, you may not be able to save enough money for the future or invest in opportunities to grow your wealth. In summary, financial trouble is always a consequence of problems with cash flow because it can lead to inadequate funds to meet your financial obligations, save for the future, or invest in opportunities.

Creating a Budget

You can use your cash flow statement to help you produce a personal budget by analyzing your income and expenses, setting realistic and achievable budget goals, and tracking your spending to make sure that you are staying on track. By using your cash flow statement and budget together, you can gain greater control over your personal finances and achieve your financial goals. To create a budget to improve your cash flow, you can follow these steps:

1. Start by reviewing your cash flow statement to understand your current income and expenses. This will help you identify areas where you can cut costs or increase your income.
2. Set realistic and achievable budget goals, such as reducing your expenses, or increasing your income.
3. Create a budget that outlines all your income and expenses for each month. Your budget should include your fixed expenses, such as rent or mortgage payments, and your variable expenses, such as groceries and entertainment. You may be able to make one monthly budget. However, you may need to create several different monthly budgets if your income and expense change dramatically during the year.
4. Use your budget monthly to track your spending and make sure that you are staying on track with your financial goals.
5. Regularly review your budget and adjust as needed. This will help you stay on top of your cash flow and make sure that you are achieving your financial goals.

By creating a budget to improve your cash flow, you can gain greater control over your personal finances and make progress towards achieving your financial goals. A budget is a powerful tool that can help you manage your money, reduce your expenses, increase your income, and save for the future. By creating a budget and sticking to it, you can improve your cash flow and achieve financial stability and success.

A budget is like a cash flow statement that you would like to achieve in the future. It is an "ideal" or "imagined" cash flow. Just like a cash flow statement, a budget includes your fixed expenses, such as rent or mortgage payments, and your variable expenses, such as groceries and entertainment. A budget also, however, implicitly recognizes your financial goals, such as saving a certain amount of money each month by reducing your expenses. By creating a budget, you can plan for how you want to manage your money in the future and achieve your financial goals. In this way, a budget is like a cash flow statement that you would like to achieve in the future.

EXAMPLE BUDGET TO INCREASE CASH FLOW

FOR THE MONTH OF JANUARY

INCOME	
Salary:	$3,500
Investment Income:	200
Total Income:	**$3,700**

EXPENSES	
Rent:	$1,000
Food:	350
Utilities:	150
Transportation:	250
Entertainment:	80
Total Expenses:	**$1,830**
NET CASH FLOW:	**$1,870**

In this budget, I reduced the food, transportation, and entertainment expenses by a modest amount. This allowed for more money to be available for savings or other expenses, leading to an improved net cash flow by $120 per month (or $1,440 per year).

Developing a plan to achieve your goals

To link your budget plan to your financial goals, you can use your budget as a tool to help you make decisions about how to allocate your money. For example, if one of your financial goals is to save for a down payment on a home, you can include a savings category in your budget and set aside a specific amount each month towards that goal. You can also track your progress towards your goal by comparing your actual savings to your budgeted amount. By regularly reviewing and adjusting your budget, you can ensure that your spending aligns with your financial goals and helps you achieve them. A good plan of action for developing a budget to meet your financial goals starts with estimating how much you need to save for each goal: This can involve doing research to find out how much your goals will cost, such as how much a down payment on a house might be, or how much you need to save for retirement. Many free online tools are available for this purpose, and they are relatively easy to use.

As for whether you should start with a timeframe for achieving your goals or let the amount dictate the timeframe, it can be helpful to do both. Start by setting a timeframe for each goal and then work backwards to determine how much you need to save each month to reach your goals within that timeframe. This can help you create a realistic plan for achieving your goals. At the same time, you should also be flexible and adjust your plan if necessary. For example, if you find that you are not able to save as much as you had hoped, you may need to adjust your budget and extend the timeframe for achieving your goals.

Tracking your progress and adjusting your plan

Tracking progress and regularly adjusting a personal budget is important because it can help you stay on track with your financial goals and avoid overspending. By regularly reviewing your budget and comparing it to your actual expenses, you can identify areas where you may be spending more or less than you had planned. This information can then be used to make adjustments to your budget plan as needed, in order to stay within your desired spending limits and avoid over- or under-spending in different areas.

There are several reasons why you may need to adjust your budget. For example, if your income changes (either due to a raise, a bonus, or a decrease in hours worked), you will need to adjust your budget to reflect this change. Additionally, if your expenses change (such as if you move to a new home or incur unexpected medical bills), you will need to adjust your budget to account for these changes.

However, it is important not to be too eager to modify your budget when you fail to meet your goals. If you make too many changes to your budget too quickly, you may end up with a plan that is unrealistic and difficult to follow. This can lead to frustration and a lack of motivation, which can make it even harder to stick to your budget in the future. It is better to make small, gradual adjustments to your budget over time, rather than trying to make sweeping changes all at once. This can help you stay on track and achieve your financial goals in a more sustainable manner.

Here is a table that compares the budget provided previously with a hypothetical scenario in which there is overspending in the "Food" and "Transportation" categories:

EXAMPLE OF OVERSPENDING ON BUDGET

Expense	Budgeted	Actual	Difference
Rent	$1,000	$1,000	$0
Food	350	450	100
Utilities	150	150	0
Transportation	250	300	50
Entertainment	80	80	0
Total Expenses	$1,830	$1,980	$150

In this scenario, the actual amount spent on food and transportation exceeded the budgeted amounts by $100 and $50, respectively. This resulted in a total difference of $150 of overspending in the overall budget.

There could be several reasons for the overspending in these categories. For example, the person may have had unplanned expenses, such as dining out with friends or taking a trip that was not budgeted for. Alternatively, the person may have underestimated their expenses in these categories and ended up spending more than they had planned. To resolve the problems of overspending in the future, the person could try to identify the reasons for the overspending and adjust their budget plan to account for these factors. For example, if the overspending was due to unplanned expenses, the person could set aside a certain amount of money each month in a "miscellaneous" or "emergency" fund to cover unexpected expenses. This can help prevent overspending in the future and keep the budget on track. Alternatively, if the person underestimated their expenses in these categories, they could review their spending habits and make more accurate estimates in their budget plan to avoid overspending in the future.

Overcoming challenges and setbacks

There are several challenges and setbacks that people may face when trying to stick to a budget for the first time. One of the biggest challenges is accurately estimating expenses, as many people may underestimate their expenses and end up overspending. Additionally, unexpected expenses can arise that throw off a budget, and impulse buying can also make it difficult to stick to a budget. Lack of motivation and psychological roadblocks, such as feeling controlled or frustrated by the discipline of sticking to a budget, can also be challenges. Some people may feel that a budget is controlling or restrictive, and may resent the discipline and work involved in sticking to it. Others may feel disappointed or frustrated when they are unable to stick to their budget, which can lead to a lack of motivation. However, with careful planning and discipline, it is possible to overcome these challenges and achieve financial success.

Cognitive Behavioral Therapy, or CBT, is a type of self-help that can help people overcome challenges and achieve their goals. One way to use CBT principles when trying to stick to a budget is to identify and change negative thought patterns that may be hindering your ability to stick to the budget. Here are some steps you can take to use CBT to overcome challenges when trying to stick to a budget:

- Identify negative thoughts: Take some time to reflect on your thoughts and emotions when you are trying to stick to your budget. What negative thoughts or beliefs come up for you? For example, you may have thoughts like "Budgeting is too hard" or "I'll never be able to stick to this budget."
- Challenge these negative thoughts: Once you have identified your negative thought patterns, it is important to challenge them and evaluate their validity. For example, you can ask yourself questions like

"Is it really true that budgeting is too hard?" or "Is it really impossible for me to stick to this budget?"

- Reframe the negative thoughts: Once you have challenged your negative thought patterns, the next step is to reframe them in a more positive and constructive way. For example, instead of thinking "Budgeting is too hard," you could reframe this thought as "Budgeting can be challenging at times, but I am determined to make it work." This can help you approach your budget with a more positive and constructive mindset.
- Use positive self-talk: In addition to reframing your negative thoughts, it can also be helpful to use positive self-talk to motivate and encourage yourself when trying to stick to your budget. For example, you could remind yourself of your financial goals and why they are important to you, and use positive affirmations to remind yourself that you can stick to your budget.

Overall, using principles of CBT can be a helpful way to overcome the challenges and setbacks that you may face when trying to stick to a budget. By identifying and changing negative thought patterns, you can approach your budget with a more positive and constructive mindset, which can help you stay on track and achieve your financial goals.

Case studies of successful goal setting

Here are two examples of people successfully achieving their budgetary goals through careful planning and discipline:

Case Study 1: Sam

Sam is a 35-year-old accountant who has always struggled to stick to a budget. Despite his best efforts, he found that he was consistently overspending in several categories and was unable to save as much money as he would like. Determined to change his financial situation, Sam decided to seek out the help of a financial planner. The planner helped him create a detailed budget plan that was tailored to his income and expenses, and provided guidance and support to help him stick to the plan. Over time, Sam found that he was able to consistently stay within his budget and was able to save more money than he had ever been able to before.

Case Study 2: Rachel

Rachel is a 27-year-old marketing professional who recently moved to a new city. She was excited about the new opportunities in her career but was also worried about the higher cost of living in her new city. To help manage her finances, Rachel decided to create a budget plan that would allow her to save money and avoid overspending. She carefully tracked her expenses and income, and adjusted her budget as needed to stay on track. With the help of her budget plan, Rachel was able to save enough money to put a down payment on a new home and was able to enjoy her new city without worrying about overspending.

These case studies demonstrate that it is possible to achieve budgetary goals with careful planning and discipline. By creating a detailed budget plan and consistently tracking their expenses and income, both Sam and Rachel were able to successfully achieve their financial goals. Reading about people like Sam and Rachel who have successfully achieved their budgetary goals can be inspiring and motivate you to take control of your own finances. Seeing how they were able to create a budget plan and stick to it, even in the face of challenges and setbacks, can help you believe that it is possible for you to achieve your own financial goals.

Additionally, reading about their specific strategies and techniques can provide valuable insights and ideas that you can use to create your own budget plan. For example, you may be inspired by Sam's decision to seek out the help of a financial planner, or by Rachel's careful tracking of her expenses and income. These examples can help you see that there are many ways to approach budgeting and can give you the confidence and motivation to create a plan that works for you.

Being inspired by the examples of people like Sam and Rachel can help you take control of your own finances and achieve your own budgeting goals. By learning from their strategies and techniques, you can create a plan that is tailored to your own income and expenses, and work towards achieving your financial goals.

The next steps for achieving your financial goals

After discussing the importance of budgeting, the next step is to focus on creating an emergency fund. An emergency fund is a set amount of money that is set aside to cover unexpected expenses, such as medical bills, car repairs, or job loss. Having an emergency fund can provide financial stability and security and can help prevent overspending and financial stress. Establishing an emergency fund is an important step after creating a budget, as it allows you to save money and prepare for unexpected expenses.

Planning for Disaster

I remember the day my car stereo was stolen like it was yesterday. I had just finished a long day at work and was looking forward to driving home and relaxing with some music. But as I approached my car, I noticed that the window was smashed, and the stereo was gone.

I was devastated. I had spent a small fortune on that stereo and now it was gone in an instant. I was angry and frustrated. But then I remembered that I had insurance. I had purchased comprehensive coverage specifically to protect against incidents like this, and I was relieved to know that I had a safety net. I filed a claim with my insurance company and was pleasantly surprised by how easy the process was. They handled everything for me, from paying for the damages to my car to reimbursing me for the cost of the stolen stereo.

However, I still had to pay a deductible, which is the amount you are required to pay out of pocket before your insurance kicks in. That's when I was glad to have an emergency fund. I had set aside a small amount of money specifically for unexpected expenses, and I was able to use that money to pay for my deductible.

I learned that insurance and an emergency fund are essential parts of financial planning. They protect you from unexpected disasters and help you recover from financial losses. It's worth the investment to have that security and peace of mind.

Building an emergency fund

An emergency fund is a crucial component of a strong financial plan. To build an emergency fund, start by setting a goal for the amount you want to save as part of your budget. A general rule of thumb is to save enough to cover three to six months of living expenses. Next, determine how much you can afford to save each month and automate your savings by setting up a direct deposit or regular transfer from your checking account to a savings account designated for your emergency fund. Avoid dipping into your emergency fund unless it's for a true emergency, such as a job loss or unexpected medical expense. It's also important to regularly review your emergency fund and adjust your savings plan as needed to ensure that you have a sufficient safety net.

Identifying potential financial disasters and their impacts

To identify potential financial disasters and their potential impacts, it is helpful to take a systematic and organized approach. To do this, you can start by making a list of potential financial disasters that could affect you, such as job loss, medical expenses, natural disasters, or major home repairs. Next, evaluate the likelihood and potential impact of each disaster. This may involve considering the likelihood of losing your job and the potential impact on your financial situation, as well as the likelihood and impact of natural disasters or major home repairs in your area. Once you have identified and prioritized potential financial disasters based on likelihood and impact, you can then develop a plan to prepare for each one. This may include creating an emergency fund, purchasing insurance, or developing a plan to find a new job if necessary.

Identifying Common Risks

Below is a table that outlines the common risks you may face in your financial future. Creating a table that is unique to your situation, along with best-guess probabilities for each event, can be helpful in securing your financial future.

10 YR. RISKS TO YOUR FINANCIAL FUTURE

Financial Disaster	% Likely	Possible Mitigation Measures
Job Loss	20	Create an emergency fund, update your resume and job search skills, network with potential employers
Medical Expenses	15	Purchase health insurance, create an emergency fund, save receipts for medical expenses to be used as a tax deduction
Natural Disasters	10	Purchase insurance, create an emergency fund, develop a disaster preparedness plan
Major Home Repairs	5	Create an emergency fund, maintain and update your home to prevent potential problems, consider purchasing a home warranty
Loss of Income from a Business	3	Create an emergency fund, diversify your income streams, maintain a good credit score
Loss of a Significant Investment	1	Diversify your investments, research potential investments carefully, consider seeking professional financial advice
Legal Expenses	1	Purchase insurance, seek legal advice for potential legal problems, create an emergency fund
Loss of a Family Member's Income	2	Create an emergency fund, consider purchasing life insurance
Loss of Property Due to Theft or Vandalism	1	Purchase insurance, use security measures to protect your property, create an emergency fund

A table such as the one above can be useful in identifying risks and allocating efforts towards mitigating the most likely and most problematic disasters. By including estimates of the likelihood of each potential financial disaster occurring, and possible mitigation measures, a table like this can help you quickly and easily compare and evaluate the risks that you are facing. For example, using the table above, you can see that job loss has the highest likelihood of occurring, at 20%, while loss of property due to theft or vandalism has the lowest likelihood, at 1%. This information can help you prioritize your efforts and focus on preparing for the disasters that are most likely to occur.

Additionally, the table can also help you identify potential mitigation measures that you can take to reduce the likelihood or impact of potential financial disasters. For example, if you are concerned about the potential impact of medical expenses, you can see that purchasing health insurance and creating an emergency fund are possible mitigation measures. This information can help you develop a plan to prepare for financial disasters and protect your financial security.

A table such as the one above can be useful in identifying risks and allocating efforts towards mitigating the most likely and most problematic disasters. By providing information about the likelihood and potential mitigation measures for each potential disaster, a table like this can help you make more informed decisions about how to prepare for financial disasters and protect your financial security.

Protecting your assets and income in case of financial disasters

To protect your assets and income in case of financial disasters, there are several steps you can take. Here are some potential strategies for protecting your assets and income. Several of these steps we have discussed before, but are worth revisiting:

- Create an emergency fund: One of the most important things you can do to protect your assets and income in case of financial disasters is to create an emergency fund. An emergency fund is a set amount of money that is set aside to cover unexpected expenses, such as medical bills, car repairs, or job loss. Having an emergency fund can provide financial stability and security, and can help prevent overspending and financial stress.
- Purchase insurance: Another strategy for protecting your assets and income in case of financial disasters is to purchase insurance. There are many different types of insurance that can protect you against potential financial disasters, such as health insurance, life insurance, homeowners' insurance, and car insurance. By purchasing insurance, you can reduce the potential impact of financial disasters, and help protect your assets and income.

- Develop a plan to find a new job or source of income: If you were to lose your job or source of income due to a financial disaster, it is important to have a plan in place to find a new job or source of income. This could include things like updating your resume, networking with potential employers, or developing new skills that could be valuable in the job market. By having a plan in place, you can reduce the potential impact of job loss or income loss and help protect your financial security.

In a later chapter, we will discuss in more detail diversifying sources of income. This will be an important step in creating financial security, since you will be less dependent on your principal source of income, such as your job or business, in case these sources dry up.

Maintaining and updating your emergency fund plan over time

It is important to continually update your emergency fund plan over time because your circumstances and financial situation can change. For example, your income, job security, health, family composition, and life-style expectations can all affect the size of the emergency fund that you need, and the investments that might be appropriate for that fund.

For example, if your income increases, you may need a larger emergency fund to cover potential expenses. Alternatively, if your job security decreases or you experience a health crisis, you may need a larger emergency fund to provide financial stability and security. Additionally, if your family composition changes or your life-style expectations change, you may need to adjust your emergency fund accordingly.

Furthermore, the investments that are appropriate for your emergency fund can also change over time. For example, if you are young and have many years until retirement, you may be able to take on more risk in your investments, and may be able to invest your emergency fund in higher-risk, higher-return assets. However, as you get older and approach retirement, you may want to reduce the risk in your investments and may need to invest your emergency fund in more conservative assets.

It is important to continually update your emergency fund plan over time to account for changes in your circumstances and financial situation. By regularly reviewing and updating your emergency fund plan, you can ensure that you have the financial stability and security that you need, and that your emergency fund is invested in a way that is appropriate for your situation.

Case studies and examples of successful emergency fund planning

Here are a couple of case studies of successful planning and use of emergency funds:

Case Study 1: Sam

Sam is a 35-year-old marketing manager who lives in a small city. When he first started his career, he did not have much money saved, and did not have an emergency fund. However, after several years of working and saving, he decided to start an emergency fund, and set a goal of saving $10,000.

To achieve this goal, Sam created a budget and carefully tracked his spending. He identified areas where he could save money and set aside a portion of his income each month to build up his emergency fund. He also sought the help of a financial planner, who provided valuable advice and guidance on how to invest his emergency fund.

After several years of saving and investing, Sam was able to reach his goal of saving $10,000 in his emergency fund. This provided him with financial stability and security, and allowed him to feel more confident and in control of his finances. When he was laid off from his job a few years later, he was able to use his emergency fund to cover his expenses while he searched for a new job. Thanks to his careful planning and use of an emergency fund, Sam was able to weather the financial storm and emerge stronger and more financially secure.

Case Study 2: Rachel

Rachel is a 28-year-old teacher who lives in a large city. She grew up in a financially unstable household and did not have much experience with budgeting or saving money. However, after finishing college and starting her career, Rachel decided to take control of her finances and create an emergency fund.

Rachel started by creating a budget and carefully tracking her income and expenses. She identified areas where she could save money and set aside a portion of her income each month to build up her emergency fund. She also sought the help of a financial planner, who provided valuable advice and guidance on how to invest her emergency fund.

After several years of saving and investing, Rachel was able to reach her goal of saving $5,000 in her emergency fund. When she was hit with unexpected medical expenses a few years later, she was able to use her emergency fund to cover the costs, without having to take on additional debt or sacrifice her financial goals. Thanks to her careful planning and use of an emergency fund, Rachel was able to overcome a difficult financial situation and continue to build a secure financial future.

The stories of Sam and Rachel can be used as inspiration for others who are looking to create and use an emergency fund. Both Sam and Rachel faced challenges and setbacks in their financial journeys, but they were able to overcome these challenges by carefully planning and using an emergency fund. Their stories show that with determination, discipline, and the right tools, anyone can create and use an emergency fund to protect their financial security and achieve their financial goals.

Tips for reducing expenses and increasing income

There are many ways to reduce expenses and increase income that can be helpful in saving for an emergency fund and increasing financial stability. Here are a few examples:

Reduce or eliminate unnecessary expenses: Take a close look at your spending habits and identify areas where you can cut back or eliminate expenses. For example, you might be able to save money by reducing your entertainment expenses, cutting back on dining out, or cancelling subscriptions that you don't use. By reducing unnecessary expenses, you can free up more money to save for your emergency fund and increase your financial stability.

Increase your income: In addition to reducing expenses, you can also increase your income to save for your emergency fund and increase your financial stability. There are many ways to increase your income, such as asking for a raise at work, taking on additional work or a side hustle, or starting a small business. By increasing your income, you can increase the amount of money that you have available to save for your emergency fund and improve your financial situation.

There are many ways to reduce expenses and increase income that can be helpful in saving for an emergency fund and increasing financial stability. By reducing unnecessary expenses and increasing your income, you can take control of your finances and build a secure financial future. We will look more in depth at ways to increase your earnings in a future chapter on diversifying your income.

Savings Regularly and Investing Wisely

had always dreamed of traveling to Europe. The rich history, stunning architecture, and delicious cuisine all called to me, and I knew I had to experience it for myself. But as a young professional, I didn't have a lot of money saved up and I wasn't sure how I would be able to afford such an expensive trip. That's when I decided to start saving. I set a goal for myself to save a certain amount each month and I made a budget to help me stick to it. I cut back on unnecessary expenses, like eating out and buying new clothes, and put that money towards my travel fund instead.

It wasn't always easy, and there were times when I was tempted to splurge on something else. But I stayed focused on my goal and kept putting money aside. Slowly but surely, my travel fund began to grow. I was able to save enough money to cover the cost of flights, accommodation, and activities. I was thrilled that I had been able to make my dream a reality.

When the day finally came to go on my trip, I was so grateful for the discipline and planning that had made it possible. I had an amazing time exploring all that Europe had to offer and I came home with memories that would last a lifetime. I learned that with a little bit of discipline and planning, you can achieve your financial goals. Whether it's saving for a trip overseas or something else, it's possible to make your dreams a reality if you set your mind to it.

The importance of having a savings plan

It is important to have a savings plan for several reasons. First, having a savings plan can help you prepare for unexpected expenses and emergencies, such as medical bills, car repairs, or job loss. By setting aside money in a savings account, you can have access to funds when you need them and avoid going into debt to cover unexpected costs. Second, a savings plan can help you achieve your financial goals, such as saving for a down payment on a house, paying for a child's education, or retiring comfortably. By setting aside money on a regular basis, you can build up your savings and reach your goals more quickly. Third, a savings plan can provide peace of mind and financial security. By having a plan in place and regularly saving money, you can feel more confident and in control of your financial situation. This can help reduce stress and anxiety, and allow you to focus on other aspects of your life.

Traditional savings accounts

A traditional savings account is a type of bank account that allows you to save money and earn interest on your balance. Some benefits of traditional savings accounts include:

- Safety: Savings accounts are FDIC-insured, meaning your money is backed by the government up to $250,000 per depositor.
- Accessibility: Savings accounts are liquid, which means you can access your money whenever you need it. Most banks and credit unions offer online and mobile banking options, so you can easily check your balance and make withdrawals from anywhere.
- Earnings: While the interest rates on traditional savings accounts are generally lower than other types of investments, they are still a safe and reliable way to earn a small return on your money.

Some drawbacks of traditional savings accounts include:

- Low interest rates: As mentioned, traditional savings accounts typically offer lower interest rates compared to other types of investments.
- Limited use: Savings accounts are generally intended for short-term savings, so if you are looking to save for a long-term goal, you may be better off with a different type of investment.

Despite these drawbacks, traditional savings accounts can still be a useful part of a savings plan, particularly if you are looking for a safe and easily accessible place to store your emergency fund or save for a short-term goal.

High-yield savings accounts and money market accounts

Money market accounts and high-yield savings accounts are both types of bank accounts that offer higher interest rates than traditional savings accounts. However, there are a few key differences between the two. Money market accounts and high-yield savings accounts often have similar interest rates, but money market account rates may be slightly higher on average. Money market accounts typically offer check-writing and debit card capabilities, while high-yield savings accounts generally do not. Money market accounts typically invest in short-term, low-risk securities such as certificates of deposit, treasury bills, and commercial paper, which tend to be less volatile than other types of investments. Nevertheless, their value can still go down with deteriorating market conditions.

Some benefits of high-yield accounts include:

- Higher interest rates: As the name suggests, high-yield accounts offer higher interest rates than traditional savings accounts, which can help your money grow faster.
- Safety: Like traditional savings accounts, high-yield accounts are FDIC-insured, so your money is backed by the government up to $250,000 per depositor. Money market mutual funds, often held outside banks, are not insured, so it is important to note which type of account you are opening.
- Accessibility: High-yield accounts are liquid, which means you can access your money whenever you need it. Most banks and credit unions offer online and mobile banking options, so you can easily check your balance and make withdrawals from anywhere.

Some drawbacks of high-yield accounts include:

- Balance requirements: Some high-yield accounts may have minimum balance requirements to qualify for the higher interest rate. If you cannot maintain the required balance, you may not earn the higher rate.
- Limited use: Like traditional savings accounts, high-yield accounts are generally intended for short-term savings, so if you are looking to save for a long-term goal, you may be better off with a different type of investment with a higher long-term return.

High-yield accounts can be a good option for those who are looking for a safe and easily accessible place to save their money and earn a higher return than what is offered by traditional savings accounts. However, it is important to carefully compare the interest rates and account requirements of different high-yield savings accounts to find the one that best meets your needs.

Certificate of deposit (CD) accounts

A certificate of deposit (CD) is a type of deposit account offered by banks and credit unions that pays a fixed rate of interest for a set period of time. CDs are a low-risk investment because they are FDIC-insured and have a fixed rate of return, which means you know exactly how much interest you will earn on your investment. CDs may be a good option for those who are looking for a safe and secure way to save and earn a fixed rate of return on their money. They can be particularly useful for those who have a specific savings goal in mind, such as saving for a down payment on a home or saving for retirement.

One potential disadvantage of CDs is that they usually have a fixed term, which means you must leave your money in the account for a specific period of time in order to earn the full interest rate. If you need to withdraw your money before the end of the term, you may have to pay a penalty. CDs also generally offer lower interest rates than other types of investments, so they may not be the best option for those who are looking for the highest possible return on their money. Whether a CD is a good investment option for you will depend on your specific financial goals and risk tolerance. It is important to carefully consider the terms, fees, and interest rates of different CDs before investing in one, and to choose a CD with a term that aligns with your savings goals.

Individual retirement accounts (IRAs)

An individual retirement account (IRA) is a type of investment account that is designed to help you save for retirement. IRAs are offered by banks, brokerage firms, and other financial institutions, and they allow you to invest in a wide range of assets such as stocks, bonds, mutual funds, and exchange-traded funds (ETFs). There are several types of IRAs, including traditional IRAs, Roth IRAs, and SEP IRAs.

A 401(k) plan is a type of retirement savings plan offered by employers to their employees. Like IRAs, 401(k) plans allow you to save and invest for retirement, but they are sponsored by employers rather than being offered by financial institutions. 401(k) plans often offer a variety of investment options, and many employers offer matching contributions as an incentive for their employees to save for retirement.

There are a few key differences between IRAs and 401(k) plans:

- Eligibility: Anyone can open and contribute to an IRA, regardless of whether they are employed. 401(k) plans, on the other hand, are only available to employees of participating companies.
- Contribution limits: The annual contribution limits for IRAs are generally lower than those for 401(k) plans.
- Tax treatment: Traditional IRAs and 401(k) plans offer tax-deferred growth, which means your investments can grow tax-free until you withdraw them in retirement. Roth IRAs and Roth 401(k) plans, on the other hand, offer tax-free growth, which means you pay taxes on your contributions upfront, but your investments can grow tax-free.
- Distribution options: With an IRA, you have more flexibility in terms of when and how you can withdraw your money in retirement. 401(k) plans may have stricter rules regarding distributions.

Whether an IRA or a 401(k) plan is a better option for you will depend on your specific financial situation and goals. It is generally considered a good idea to take advantage of any employer-sponsored retirement plan, such as a 401(k), if it is available to you. This is because employer-sponsored plans often offer a range of benefits, including the potential for employer matching contributions, a wider range of investment options, and sometimes even a vesting schedule for employer contributions.

However, whether a 401(k) is a better retirement plan than an IRA will depend on your specific financial situation and goals. For example, if you have already maxed out your contributions to your 401(k) and are looking for additional ways to save for retirement, an IRA may be a good option.

Or, if you are self-employed or do not have access to a 401(k) plan, an IRA may be the only retirement savings option available to you.

Health savings accounts (HSAs)

A health savings account (HSA) is a tax-advantaged savings account that can be used to pay for qualified medical expenses. HSAs are often paired with high-deductible health plans (HDHPs) and are intended to help individuals and families save money on their healthcare costs.

There are several reasons why someone might want to consider opening an HSA:

- Tax benefits: Contributions to an HSA are tax-deductible, and the money in the account grows tax-free. Withdrawals for qualified medical expenses are also tax-free.
- Flexibility: An HSA can be used to pay for a wide range of qualified medical expenses, including deductibles, copays, and prescription drugs.
- Portability: An HSA is portable, meaning it stays with the individual even if they change jobs or health insurance plans.

Potential for long-term savings: Because the money in an HSA grows tax-free and can be used to pay for qualified medical expenses in the future, it can be a good way to save for future healthcare costs.

There are also several reasons why someone might want to save their money elsewhere:

- Limited eligibility: To contribute to an HSA, an individual must be enrolled in an HDHP. If an individual is not enrolled in an HDHP or is not eligible to contribute to an HSA due to other circumstances (e.g., Medicare eligibility), they may not be able to open an HSA.
- Contribution limits: There are annual limits on how much can be contributed to an HSA. These limits may not be sufficient for individuals with high healthcare costs.
- Potential for penalty: If an HSA is used for non-qualified medical expenses, the individual may be subject to a tax penalty.

Education savings accounts (ESAs)

An education savings account (ESA) is a tax-advantaged account that can be used to save for a child's education expenses, including tuition, fees, and certain other education-related expenses. There are several types of ESAs, including Coverdell Education Savings Accounts (Coverdell ESAs) and 529 plans.

There are several reasons why someone might want to consider opening an ESA:

- Tax benefits: Contributions to an ESA may be tax-deductible or may be eligible for tax credits, depending on the type of account and the individual's tax situation. Earnings in the account grow tax-free, and withdrawals for qualified education expenses are tax-free.
- Flexibility: ESAs can be used to pay for a wide range of qualified education expenses, including tuition, fees, books, and supplies. Depending on the type of account, they may also be used to pay for certain education-related expenses, such as room and board.
- Potential for long-term savings: Because the money in an ESA grows tax-free and can be used to pay for qualified education expenses in the future, it can be a good way to save for a child's education.
- Control: With an ESA, the individual has control over how the money is invested and used.

There are also several considerations to keep in mind when deciding whether an ESA is right for an individual:

- Limited eligibility: To contribute to an ESA, an individual must meet certain income and other eligibility requirements.
- Contribution limits: There are annual limits on how much can be contributed to an ESA. These limits may not be sufficient for individuals with high education costs.
- Potential for penalty: If an ESA is used for non-qualified education expenses, the individual may be subject to a tax penalty.
- Other savings options: There are other savings options available, such as 529 plans and custodial accounts, that may offer similar tax benefits and be more suitable for an individual's financial situation.

Business savings accounts

A business savings account is a financial product that allows a business to set aside and grow its surplus cash. Businesses can use a business savings account to save money for short-term or long-term goals, such as purchasing inventory, paying taxes, or expanding the business. A business savings account can provide a secure place to store surplus cash and protect it from loss or theft. Many business savings accounts offer a higher interest rate than a traditional checking account, which means the business can earn more on its money over time. Businesses can typically access the money in their business savings account relatively easily through online banking or by visiting a branch, which can be useful for managing cash flow or paying unexpected expenses. A business savings account can help a business keep its operating funds separate from its savings, which can make it easier to track the business's financial performance and plan for the future. Like personal savings accounts, business savings accounts are typically insured by the Federal Deposit Insurance Corporation (FDIC) up to certain limits, which can provide added peace of mind for the business owner. However, some business savings accounts may charge fees for things like account maintenance or account activity and may have minimum balance requirements that must be met in order to avoid fees or earn the highest interest rate. It is important for businesses to carefully consider their financial needs and goals before deciding whether a business savings account is the right choice for them. A financial advisor or banker can help a business owner evaluate the available options and make an informed decision.

The importance of diversification

Diversification is the practice of investing in a variety of assets in order to spread risk and potentially increase returns. When an investor diversifies their portfolio, they are spreading their investments across different asset classes, sectors, and geographic regions in order to reduce the overall risk of their portfolio. Diversification can be an effective risk management tool, as it can reduce the risk of suffering significant losses due to the performance of a single investment or asset class. It can also potentially lead to higher returns over the long term by taking advantage of the different return characteristics of each asset class. Diversification also gives an investor flexibility in their portfolio, as it may allow them to weather market downturns and take advantage of opportunities as they arise. However, it's important to note that diversification does not guarantee a profit or protect against loss, and investors should consider their specific financial goals, risk tolerance, and investment time horizon when determining the appropriate level of diversification for their portfolio.

Different asset classes and their characteristics

There are several different asset classes that individuals can include in their investment portfolio:

- Stocks: Also known as equities, stocks represent ownership in a company. When an individual buys stocks, they are essentially buying a share of the company and becoming a shareholder. Stocks can provide the potential for high returns, but also come with higher risk and volatility.
- Bonds: Bonds are essentially loans made by an investor to a borrower, such as a corporation or government. The borrower agrees to pay the investor a fixed rate of interest over a set period of time and to return the principal at maturity. Bonds are generally considered to be less risky than stocks, but also typically provide lower returns.
- Mutual funds: Mutual funds are investment vehicles that pool the money of many investors and use it to buy a diversified portfolio of stocks, bonds, or other securities. Mutual funds are managed by professional fund managers and offer investors the opportunity to diversify their portfolio with a single investment.
- Exchange-traded funds (ETFs): ETFs are similar to mutual funds in that they offer investors the opportunity to invest in a diversified portfolio of securities. However, unlike mutual funds, ETFs are traded on stock

exchanges and can be bought and sold throughout the day. ETFs may offer lower fees than mutual funds and can provide more flexibility for investors.

- Real estate: Real estate investments can take various forms, such as owning rental properties, investing in real estate investment trusts (REITs), or purchasing land or other property for development. Real estate investments can provide the potential for high returns, but also come with risks, such as fluctuating property values and the costs of maintenance and repair.

Picking investments that do not require a lot of time and effort in managing them can be an important consideration for many individuals. Passive investments, such as index mutual funds and exchange-traded funds (ETFs), are designed to track the performance of a specific market index and generally do not require a lot of ongoing research or monitoring. Automated investing, also known as robo-advisors, are online platforms that use algorithms to create and manage investment portfolios on behalf of clients, which can be a good option for individuals who want a hands-off approach to investing. Building a diversified portfolio of investments can also help to minimize the time and effort required to manage the portfolio, as it can reduce the need to constantly monitor investments and make frequent trades. However, it's important to keep in mind that investments that require less time and effort to manage may also come with trade-offs, such as potentially lower returns or a lack of control over specific investments. It's a good idea for individuals to carefully consider their financial goals, risk tolerance, and investment time horizon before deciding which type of investments are right for them.

Strategies for diversifying your portfolio

Diversification is the practice of investing in a variety of assets to spread risk. There are several strategies and tips that can help investors diversify their portfolio: investing in a mix of asset classes, such as stocks, bonds, and real estate; diversifying within each asset class; considering geographic diversification; using low-cost, diversified investment vehicles, such as index mutual funds and exchange-traded funds (ETFs); and regularly reviewing and rebalancing the portfolio to ensure it continues to align with an investor's financial goals and risk tolerance. It's important for individuals to carefully consider their specific financial goals, risk tolerance, and investment time horizon when determining the appropriate level of diversification for their portfolio.

Being aware of scams and fraudulent investment opportunities

Scams and fraudulent investments can be difficult to detect, as they often involve sophisticated schemes designed to deceive and mislead investors. To raise your awareness of these types of investments, it's important to be wary of unsolicited offers, do your research, check the credentials of the person making the offer, be cautious of "guaranteed" returns, and be aware of common red flags, such as promises of high returns with little or no risk, pressure to act quickly, requests for personal information or upfront fees, and a lack of transparency about how the investment works. By being vigilant and doing your due diligence, you can better protect yourself from scams and fraudulent investments. There is more information on protecting yourself from scams and fraud in our final chapter.

Being self-employed is not the same as making an investment

Self-employment and investing are two distinct activities that can have different implications for an individual's financial and tax situation. It's important not to confuse these two activities, as they have different risks and potential rewards. Self-employment refers to the act of operating a business as an individual rather than as an employee. When an individual is self-employed, they are responsible for running their own business and generating their own income. They may work as a freelancer, contractor, or small business owner, and may have to handle tasks such as marketing, sales, and accounting in addition to their primary work. Investing, on the other hand, involves putting money into a financial vehicle, such as stocks, bonds, or mutual funds, with the goal of generating a return. Investing carries risks, as the value of an investment can go up or down based on market conditions. However, it also has the potential for providing returns in the form of dividends, interest, or capital appreciation.

It's important not to confuse self-employment and investing because they have different tax implications. Self-employed individuals are responsible for paying self-employment tax, which includes Social Security and Medicare taxes, on their net earnings from self-employment. They may also be eligible for tax deductions related to their business expenses. Investing, on the other hand, may generate taxable income in the form of dividends or capital gains, and investors may be subject to different tax rates depending on the type of investment and their holding period.

In summary, it's important for individuals to understand the differences between self-employment and investing and to be aware of the potential risks and rewards of each activity. Consultation with a financial advisor or tax professional can clarify the tax implications of these activities and in developing a financial plan that aligns with an individual's goals and circumstances.

The benefits of working with a financial advisor

Working with a financial advisor can provide several benefits, including professional advice, goal setting and planning, coordination of financial matters, personalized service, and peace of mind. A financial advisor can offer expert guidance on a wide range of financial topics, such as budgeting, saving, investing, and planning for retirement. They can also help you clarify your financial goals and develop a plan to achieve them. Additionally, a financial advisor can help you manage and coordinate all your financial matters, including investments, taxes, and insurance.

Financial advisors can provide personalized service and advice based on your specific financial situation, needs, and goals. Working with a financial advisor can also give you peace of mind and help you feel more confident about your financial future. It's important to choose a financial advisor that is a good fit for you and your financial needs, and to consider factors such as qualifications, experience, and fee structure when deciding.

Different types of financial advisors and their services

There are several different types of financial advisors, including financial planners, wealth managers, investment advisors, insurance agents, and retirement planning specialists. Each of these advisors provides different services, depending on their specialty and the needs of their clients. For example, financial planners may help clients create a plan to achieve their financial goals, such as saving for retirement or buying a home, and may provide advice on a wide range of financial topics. Wealth managers may provide comprehensive financial planning and asset management services to high-net-worth individuals, and may work with a team of professionals to develop and implement a financial plan. Investment advisors may provide advice on how to invest money and may manage a portfolio of investments for their clients. Insurance agents may sell insurance policies, such as life, health, and property insurance, and may help clients determine how much coverage they need, and which type of policy is best for their needs. Retirement planning specialists may help clients plan for their financial needs during retirement, including saving for retirement, choosing the right retirement account, and creating a retirement income plan. It's important to choose a financial advisor that is well-suited to your financial needs and goals.

How to find and evaluate financial advisors

When evaluating financial advisors, there are several factors you should consider finding the one that is right for you. These factors may include the advisor's qualifications, experience, fee structure, services offered, and personality and communication style. It's important to look for financial advisors who have the appropriate education and training for the services they provide, and who have experience in the areas that are most important to you. You should also understand how an advisor charges for their services and make sure the fee structure is clear and transparent. Consider the services an advisor offers and whether they meet your needs. Choose an advisor you feel comfortable working with and who communicates in a way that you understand. To find financial advisors in your area, you can ask for referrals from friends, family, or other professionals, or you can search online directories or websites such as the National Association of

Personal Financial Advisors (NAPFA) or the Financial Planning Association (FPA). You may also want to interview several advisors before deciding.

The importance of aligning your values and goals with your financial advisor

It's important that your financial advisor be aware of your values and goals because they will play a major role in shaping your financial plan and decision-making. Your values and goals will help your financial advisor understand what is most important to you and what you hope to achieve with your money. For example, if environmental sustainability is a value that is important to you, your financial advisor may recommend investments in renewable energy or socially responsible mutual funds. Similarly, if your goal is to retire early, your financial advisor can help you develop a plan to save and invest in a way that will help you reach that goal.

By understanding your values and goals, your financial advisor can provide more personalized and relevant advice, and can help you make financial decisions that are consistent with your priorities and values. This can help you feel more confident and satisfied with your financial plan, and can help you achieve your financial goals more effectively.

Considering the fees and compensation of financial advisors

It's important to look at fees and the compensation structure of potential financial advisors because the way an advisor charges for their services can impact the cost and value of their advice. Different advisors may have different fee structures, such as a flat fee, hourly rate, or percentage of assets under management. It's important to understand how an advisor charges for their services and to make sure the fee structure is clear and transparent. Some advisors may charge a percentage of the assets they manage for you, while others may charge a flat fee for their services. It's also important to consider whether an advisor's fees are reasonable and competitive, and whether they are a good value for the services they provide.

Financial advisors who are compensated for pushing particular financial investments or insurance products may have conflicts of interest that can impact the advice they provide. If an advisor is paid a commission or receives other financial incentives to sell a particular product, they may be more likely to recommend that product to their clients, even if it may not be the best fit for their needs. This can create a bias in the advice the advisor provides and may result in the advisor recommending products that are more profitable for them, rather than those that are in the best interests of the client. Additionally, financial advisors who are compensated for selling particular products may not always fully disclose the terms, fees, and risks of those products to their clients. This can make it difficult for clients to make informed decisions about their finances, and may result in clients making investments or purchasing insurance policies that are not suitable for their needs or that carry more risk than they realize.

To avoid these problems, it's important to choose a financial advisor who is transparent about their compensation and who does not have conflicts of interest that could impact the advice they provide. You may want to consider working with a fee-only financial advisor, who charges a flat fee or hourly rate for their services and does not receive commissions or other financial incentives to sell particular products. This can help ensure that the advice you receive is objective and unbiased.

It's not always possible to determine which compensation structure is best, as it will depend on your individual circumstances and needs. For example, if you have a large investment portfolio, you may be willing to pay a higher percentage-based fee for professional asset management. On the other hand, if you have a smaller portfolio or are looking for one-time financial planning advice, a flat fee or hourly rate may be more appropriate. Ultimately, the most important thing is to choose a financial advisor whose fees and compensation structure are transparent and aligned with your needs and goals. It's also a good idea to shop around and compare the fees and services of several advisors before making a decision.

Evaluating the credentials and experience of financial advisors

Here are a few quick tips for evaluating the credentials and experience of financial advisors: Look for professional designations, such as Certified Financial Planner (CFP) or Chartered Financial Analyst (CFA), that indicate the advisor has completed specific education and training requirements. Check the advisor's licensing and registration status through regulatory bodies like the Securities and Exchange Commission (SEC) or the Financial Industry Regulatory Authority (FINRA). Consider the level of experience an advisor has in the areas that are most important to you, and research the background and reputation of the financial advisory firm if applicable. You may also want to ask the financial advisor for references from past or current clients, or seek recommendations from friends, family, or other professionals. By following these tips, you can help ensure that you choose a financial advisor who is well-qualified and experienced, and who can provide the level of service and advice you need.

Asking the right questions and getting to know your financial advisor

When considering a potential financial advisor, it's important to ask a range of questions to help you determine whether they are a good fit for your needs. Here are some questions you may want to ask:

1. What are your qualifications and experience?
2. How do you charge for your services, and what is your fee structure?

3. What services do you offer, and how do you customize your services for your clients?
4. How do you communicate with your clients, and how often will we meet?
5. How do you make investment recommendations, and how do you decide which investments are appropriate for your clients?
6. How do you manage potential conflicts of interest?
7. Can you provide references from past or current clients?
8. Do you have any disciplinary actions or legal issues on your record?

Asking these questions can help you learn more about the advisor's qualifications, experience, services, and communication style, and can help you make an informed decision about whether they are the right fit for your financial needs. It's also a good idea to have a clear understanding of your own financial goals and needs before you meet with a financial advisor, so that you can ask specific questions related to your situation.

Understanding the limitations of financial advisors and when to seek additional guidance

It's important to always be the final decision maker on any investment or on considering the purchase of an insurance product. You should carefully consider the advice of your financial advisor, but ultimately you are responsible for your own financial decisions. It's a good idea to ask questions, do your own research, and potentially seek the advice of multiple advisors before making any financial decisions.

Setting up a system for tracking your investments

To set up a system for tracking your investments without taking up too much of your time, you can use online tools provided by brokerage firms or financial planning websites, create a spreadsheet using a program like Microsoft Excel or Google Sheets, or set up alerts through brokerage firms or financial planning websites to notify you of important events or changes related to your investments. By using these strategies, you can create a system that is efficient and easy to maintain, and it's a good idea to review your investments periodically to make sure they are still aligned with your financial goals and risk tolerance.

Monitoring your portfolio regularly

In general, it's a good idea to review your portfolio periodically to make sure it is still aligned with your financial goals and risk tolerance. This may mean reviewing your portfolio once a year, or more frequently if you have specific financial goals or are approaching a major life event, such as retirement. It's important to strike a balance between monitoring your portfolio too often and not monitoring it often enough. Checking your portfolio and making changes too often, known as "portfolio churning," can be costly, as it may result in you paying more in trading fees and taxes. Additionally, frequent trading may not always be in your best interests, as it can expose your portfolio to more risk and may result in you missing out on long-term returns.

On the other hand, not monitoring your portfolio often enough can also be a problem, as your financial situation and investment needs may change over time. By reviewing your portfolio periodically, you can make sure it is still aligned with your financial goals and risk tolerance, and you can make any necessary adjustments.

Evaluating the performance of your investments

There are several ways you can evaluate the performance of your investments: Compare your returns to a benchmark like the S&P 500 Index or the Bloomberg Barclays US Aggregate Bond Index, use online tools provided by brokerage firms or financial planning websites, or review your portfolio periodically to make sure it is aligned with your financial goals and risk tolerance. It is generally a good idea to consider the performance of the broader market when evaluating your investment performance, as it can provide context and help you understand how your investments are performing relative to the overall market. However, it's important to keep in mind that the performance of the broader market does not necessarily reflect the performance of your individual investments, and you should consider other factors as well.

Adjusting your investment strategy as needed

There are several key events or situations that may cause you to adjust your investment strategy. If your financial goals or circumstances change, you may need to adjust your investment strategy to ensure it is still aligned with your objectives. For example, if you are approaching retirement, you may need to shift your investments from a higher-risk, higher-return strategy to a more conservative approach. Changes in the market can also impact the performance of your investments. Economic conditions, market trends, and other external factors can all affect the value of your portfolio. If you see significant changes in the market, you may need to adjust your investment strategy to protect your portfolio or to take advantage of new opportunities.

Your risk tolerance may also change over time due to a variety of factors such as your age, financial situation, or changes in your personal circumstances. It's important to review your risk tolerance periodically and to make sure your investment strategy is aligned with your risk tolerance. This can help you manage the level of risk you are comfortable with and can help you avoid taking on more risk than you are prepared to handle.

Finally, your investment horizon, or the length of time you plan to hold your investments, may change due to factors such as your age, financial goals, or changes in your personal circumstances. If your investment horizon changes, you may need to adjust your investment strategy to reflect your new time horizon. For example, if you have a longer investment horizon, you may be able to take on more risk, as you have a longer time frame to weather market fluctuations. On the other hand, if you have a shorter investment horizon, you may need to be more conservative in your investment strategy to protect your portfolio and reduce the risk of losing money. By regularly reviewing your investment strategy and making adjustments as needed, you can help ensure that your investments are aligned with your financial goals and risk tolerance.

Reviewing and rebalancing your portfolio

Rebalancing your portfolio refers to the process of adjusting the allocation of your investments to maintain your desired level of risk and to align your portfolio with your financial goals. This may involve selling some investments and using the proceeds to buy others, or simply adding new investments to your portfolio. There are several reasons why you might want to rebalance your portfolio, such as to maintain your desired level of risk, to align your portfolio with your financial goals, or to take advantage of market opportunities.

Being aware of changes in the market and economic conditions

It's important to be aware of changes in market and economic conditions because they can impact the performance of your investments. By staying informed about market and economic trends, you can make more informed decisions about your investments and help protect your portfolio from potential risks. However, it's also important to avoid overreacting to changes in market and economic conditions. It can be tempting to make drastic changes to your portfolio in response to short-term market fluctuations, but this can be risky and may not always be in your best interests.

To avoid the temptation to overreact, it's important to have a well-thought-out investment plan that is aligned with your financial goals and risk tolerance. This can help you stay focused on your long-term objectives and avoid making impulsive decisions based on short-term market movements. It's also a good idea to diversify your portfolio and invest in a mix of different asset classes, as this can help reduce your overall portfolio risk and provide a buffer against market volatility.

Finally, it's important to remember that market and economic conditions are always changing, and it's normal for the value of your investments to fluctuate over time. By staying calm and sticking to your long-term investment plan, you can help protect your portfolio and potentially benefit from market opportunities in the long run.

Discipline and Patience Pay Off

Congratulations on completing this chapter on saving regularly and investing wisely! By following the principles discussed in this chapter, you have taken an important step towards achieving your financial goals and building a secure financial future.

By saving regularly and investing wisely, you are setting yourself up for long-term financial success. Whether you are saving for a down payment on a home, planning for retirement, or simply building a financial cushion for the future, the habits you develop now will have a significant impact on your financial well-being.

Remember, saving and investing require discipline and patience, but the rewards are well worth it. By staying focused on your financial goals and making informed decisions about your investments, you can build a strong financial foundation for yourself and your loved ones.

Keep up the good work, and don't be afraid to seek guidance from financial professionals when needed. With a solid plan and a commitment to saving and investing wisely, you can achieve your financial dreams and live a financially secure life.

Credit and Debt Management

I had always dreamed of owning a home, and when I finally saved up enough money to make a down payment, I was excited to start the process. I had heard that getting a mortgage could be challenging, especially for first-time home buyers like me, so I wasn't sure what to expect. But when I applied for a mortgage, I was pleasantly surprised. My credit rating was higher than I had expected, and I was approved for a loan with a great interest rate. I was thrilled that my financial discipline and responsible credit habits had paid off.

I was able to find a beautiful condo in a great location, and I was thrilled to finally have a place of my own. I had always loved the idea of living in a condo because of the amenities and the sense of community. Plus, I knew I would be able to save money on maintenance and yard work. I was grateful for my good credit rating and the financial discipline that had made it possible for me to achieve my dream of homeownership. It was a great feeling to know that I had worked hard to build a strong financial foundation, and it had paid off.

In this chapter, we will explore the topic of credit and debt management, and how these factors can affect your financial well-being. We will start by looking at the basics of credit, including what it is and how it works. We will also discuss the role of credit scores and credit reports in your financial life, and the importance of maintaining good credit.

Next, we will delve into the topic of managing and paying off debt. We will talk about the importance of paying off your debts on time and provide strategies for managing and reducing your debts. We will also discuss the role of budgeting and financial planning in debt management, and the potential risks and benefits of using debt consolidation or credit counseling to manage your debts.

Finally, we will provide tips for improving your credit score, and discuss the common mistakes that people make when trying to improve their credit. We will also talk about the role of credit utilization in your credit score and provide strategies for improving and repairing your credit.

This chapter will provide a comprehensive overview of the topic of credit and debt management and will equip you with the knowledge and tools you need to manage your credit and debts effectively. Understanding credit and how it affects your finances.

The Basics of Credit

In this section, we will explore the basics of credit, including what it is and how it works, the role of credit scores and credit reports in your financial life, and the importance of maintaining good credit. We will also discuss the common pitfalls of overusing credit and poor credit management, and the potential consequences of these mistakes. By the end of this section, you will have a better understanding of the basics of credit and will be equipped with the knowledge and tools you need to manage your credit wisely and achieve your financial goals.

What is credit and how does it work?

A credit score is a numerical representation of an individual's creditworthiness. It is used by lenders and creditors to evaluate an individual's credit risk, and to determine whether to approve a loan or credit application, and at what interest rate. Credit scores are calculated using algorithms that take into account various factors from an individual's credit history, such as payment history, credit utilization, and the length of their credit history. The algorithms used to calculate credit scores are proprietary and are typically developed by credit bureaus or other credit-scoring companies.

To calculate a credit score, credit bureaus and credit-scoring companies collect and analyze credit data from a variety of sources, including credit card companies, banks, and other lenders. This data is used to create a credit report, which is a detailed record of an individual's credit history. The credit report is then used to calculate a credit score, which is typically expressed as a number ranging from 300 to 850. The higher the credit score, the better an individual's creditworthiness, and the more likely they are to be approved for a loan or credit at a favorable interest rate.

The role of credit scores and credit reports in your financial life

The role of credit scores and credit reports in an individual's financial life is to provide lenders and creditors with information about an individual's creditworthiness and credit risk. Credit scores and credit reports help lenders and creditors make informed decisions about whether to approve a loan or credit application, and at what interest rate. Credit scores and credit reports can also be used by individuals to manage their own finances and achieve their financial goals. For example, an individual can use their credit score to determine whether they are likely to be approved for a loan or credit card, and at what interest rate. This can help them make informed decisions about whether to apply for credit, and what type of credit to apply for.

Additionally, credit reports can be used by individuals to monitor their credit history, and to identify errors or potential issues that may be affecting their credit score. By regularly reviewing their credit report, an individual can take steps to improve their credit score and their financial situation.

Errors in credit reports

Errors in credit reports are not uncommon. According to a study by the Federal Trade Commission, one in four consumers had errors on their credit reports that were corrected by the credit bureaus after they were disputed. You do not need to pay money to examine your credit report. Under federal law, you are entitled to one free credit report from each of the three major credit bureaus (Equifax, Experian, and TransUnion) every 12 months. You can request your free credit report online, by phone, or by mail.

If you find errors on your credit report, you have the right to dispute the errors with the credit bureaus. You can do this by contacting the credit bureau directly and providing them with documentation or evidence that the information on your credit report is incorrect. In the US, the credit bureau is then required to investigate the error, and to correct any inaccurate or incomplete information on your credit report.

The rights to inspect and correct credit reports are not unique to the United States and are generally recognized in many countries around the world. In the European Union, for example, the General Data Protection Regulation (GDPR) provides individuals with the right to access, rectify, erase, or restrict the processing of their personal data, including credit data. This means that individuals in the EU have the right to request a copy of their credit report, and to challenge and correct any inaccurate or incomplete information on their credit report. Similarly, in Canada, the Personal Information Protection and Electronic Documents Act (PIPEDA) gives individuals the right to access their personal information, including credit information, held by organizations. This allows individuals in Canada to request a copy of their credit report, and to correct any errors or inaccuracies on their credit report.

The importance of maintaining good credit

Maintaining a good credit rating is important because it can have a significant impact on your financial well-being. A good credit rating can make it easier for you to access credit, and can help you get approved for loans and credit cards at favorable interest rates. This can be especially important if you need to borrow money for large purchases, such as a house or a car, or if you want to establish a good credit history for future financial goals.

Additionally, a good credit rating can also save you money in the long run. By getting approved for loans and credit cards at favorable interest rates, you can avoid paying higher interest rates and fees, which can add up over time. This can help you save money and improve your overall financial situation. Furthermore, a good credit rating can also provide you with financial flexibility and security. By having a good credit rating, you can be more confident that you will be able to access credit when you need it, whether it's to cover an unexpected expense or to take advantage of a financial opportunity. This can provide you with peace of mind and can help you feel more secure about your financial future.

The dangers of overusing credit and the consequences of poor credit management

The dangers of overusing credit, and the consequences of poor credit management, include falling into debt, damaging your credit score, and increasing your risk of financial stress and financial problems. Overusing credit means borrowing more money than you can afford to pay back or using credit to finance a lifestyle that you cannot afford. This can lead to falling into debt, where you are unable to make your monthly credit card or loan payments, and your debts start to pile up. This can be a stressful and overwhelming situation, and can put a strain on your relationships and your mental health.

Additionally, overusing credit and poor credit management can also damage your credit score. A low credit score can make it difficult for you to access credit, and can result in you being approved for loans and credit cards at higher interest rates. This can cost you more money in the long run and can make it harder for you to achieve your financial goals. Furthermore, overusing credit and poor credit management can increase your risk of financial stress and financial problems. By borrowing more money than you can afford to pay back, you may be putting your financial future at risk. This can lead to financial insecurity and can make it difficult for you to achieve your financial goals, such as buying a house or retiring comfortably.

Managing and paying off debt

Next, we will explore the topic of managing and paying off debt. We will talk about the importance of paying off your debts on time and provide strategies for managing and reducing your debts. We will also discuss the role of budgeting and financial planning in debt management, and the potential risks and benefits of using debt consolidation or credit counseling to manage your debts. By the end of this section, you will have a better understanding of how to manage and pay off your debts, and will be equipped with the tools and knowledge you need to achieve financial freedom and stability.

The importance of paying off your debts on time

The importance of paying off debt on time cannot be overstated. By paying off your debts on time, you can avoid late fees and penalties, which can add up quickly and make it more difficult to pay off your debts. Additionally, paying off your debts on time can help you maintain a good credit score, which can make it easier for you to access credit in the future, and can help you get approved for loans and credit cards at favorable interest rates. This can save you money in the long run and can help you achieve your financial goals.

Furthermore, paying off your debts on time can also provide you with peace of mind and financial security. By avoiding late fees and penalties, and maintaining a good credit score, you can be confident that you are managing your finances responsibly, and that you are on track to achieving financial freedom and stability. This can help you feel more in control of your finances and can help you avoid financial stress and financial problems.

Strategies for managing and reducing your debts

There are several strategies that can be helpful in managing and reducing your debts. These include creating a budget and a debt repayment plan, prioritizing high-interest debts, and exploring options for consolidating or refinancing your debts. Creating a budget and a debt repayment plan can help you manage your debts more effectively, by giving you a clear picture of your income, expenses, and debts. This can help you identify areas where you can cut expenses and can help you prioritize which debts to pay off first. By creating a budget and a debt repayment plan, you can take control of your finances, and can make a plan for achieving your financial goals.

Additionally, prioritizing high-interest debts can be a helpful strategy for managing and reducing your debts. By paying off your high-interest debts first, you can save money on interest, and can make progress towards paying off your debts faster. This can be especially important for credit card debts, which often have high interest rates, and can be difficult to pay off. By prioritizing high-interest debts, you can make your debt repayment efforts more effective, and can save money in the long run.

Furthermore, exploring options for consolidating or refinancing your debts can also be a helpful strategy for managing and reducing your debts. By consolidating your debts, you can combine multiple debts into one loan, which can make it easier to manage your debts, and can potentially reduce your interest rates and monthly payments. By refinancing your debts, you can replace your existing debts with a new loan, which can also potentially reduce your interest rates and monthly payments. Both options can make it easier to manage and pay off your debts and can help you save money in the long run.

Here is an example of a debt repayment plan:

1. Create a budget to identify your income, expenses, and debts. See the prior chapter for details on how to create a personal budget.
2. List your debts in order of interest rate, from highest to lowest.
3. For each debt, calculate your monthly minimum payment, and your total interest charges over the life of the loan.
4. Set a goal for paying off each debt within a certain timeframe, such as within one year for high-interest debts, and within three years for lower-interest debts.

5. Determine how much extra money you can put towards your debts each month, beyond your minimum payments, and allocate this money to your highest-interest debt first.
6. As you pay off each debt, roll the extra money you were putting towards that debt into your next-highest-interest debt, and continue this process until all your debts are paid off.
7. Monitor your progress regularly, and adjust your plan as needed.

This is an example of a debt repayment plan that can be helpful in managing and reducing your debts. By creating a budget, prioritizing your debts, setting goals, and allocating extra money towards your debts, you can plan for paying off your debts, and can take control of your finances. By following this plan, and adjusting as needed, you can achieve your financial goals and achieve financial freedom.

The potential risks and benefits of using debt consolidation or credit counseling to manage your debts

Debt consolidation and credit counseling can both be useful tools for managing debts, but they also have potential risks and benefits that you should be aware of. One potential benefit of using debt consolidation is that it can make it easier to manage your debts. By consolidating your debts into one loan, you can reduce the number of monthly payments you have to make and can potentially reduce your interest rates and monthly payments. This can make it easier to manage your debts and can help you save money in the long run.

However, there are also potential risks to using debt consolidation. One risk is that consolidating your debts can extend the length of your loan and can increase the total amount of interest you pay over the life of the loan. This can make it more difficult to pay off your debts in the long run and can increase the total cost of your debts.

Another potential benefit of using credit counseling is that it can provide you with expert advice and guidance on managing your debts. A credit counselor can help you create a budget, develop a debt repayment plan, and negotiate with your creditors to reduce your interest rates and monthly payments. This can be especially helpful if you are struggling to manage your debts on your own, and can provide you with the support and guidance you need to get back on track.

However, there are also potential risks to using credit counseling. One risk is that credit counseling can be expensive and can require you to pay fees for the services provided. This can add to your overall debt burden and can make it more difficult to pay off your debts in the long run. Additionally, some credit counselors may not be reputable or trustworthy, and may not provide you with the best advice or guidance. This can be especially true of credit counselors who charge high fees, or who promise unrealistic results.

The difference between positive and negative debt

Debt is not always bad, and can be a useful tool for managing your finances, if used wisely. In general, debt can be divided into two categories: positive debt and negative debt.

Positive debt is debt that is used to finance investments that have the potential to increase in value over time, or to generate income. Examples of positive debt include student loans, mortgages for rental property, and small business loans. These types of debt can help you finance investments that can improve your financial situation and can provide you with the funds you need to achieve your financial goals.

Negative debt, on the other hand, is debt that is used to finance consumption or expenses that do not have the potential to increase in value or generate income. Examples of negative debt include credit card debt, personal loans, and payday loans. These types of debt can be costly and can make it difficult for you to pay off your debts.

In short, debt is not always bad, and can be a useful tool for managing your finances, if used wisely. By understanding the difference between positive and negative debt, and by using debt responsibly, you can make informed decisions about borrowing, and can use debt to your advantage, to achieve your financial goals.

Tips for improving your credit score

A good credit score is an important part of your financial life, and can affect your ability to get a loan, a credit card, or even a job. A good credit score can also save you money, by helping you qualify for lower interest rates on loans and credit cards. Therefore, it's important to take steps to improve your credit score, and to maintain a good credit rating. In this section, we will provide some tips for improving your credit score, and for maintaining a good credit rating. By following these tips, you can improve your credit score, and can take control of your finances.

How to build and maintain good credit

Building and maintaining good credit is an important part of managing your finances. Here are a few tips to help you get started:

- Make sure you pay your bills on time. This is the single most important factor in determining your credit score, so it's crucial to pay all of your bills on time, every time. Set up automatic payments if you need to, and make sure you have enough money in your account to cover your bills.
- Keep your credit card balances low. High balances on your credit cards can hurt your credit score, so try to keep your balances below 30% of your credit limit. If you have multiple credit cards, spread your balances out evenly to avoid having one card maxed out.
- Don't open too many new credit accounts at once. Each time you apply for a new credit card or loan, it can cause a small, temporary drop in

your credit score. To avoid this, try to limit the number of new accounts you open, and don't apply for more credit than you need.

- Check your credit report regularly. Your credit report contains detailed information about your credit history, and it's a good idea to review it regularly to make sure everything is accurate. You can request a free copy of your credit report from each of the three major credit bureaus (Equifax, Experian, and TransUnion) once a year.
- Consider getting a secured credit card. If you have bad credit or no credit history, a secured credit card can be a good way to build or rebuild your credit. With a secured card, you deposit money into an account and the credit card issuer extends a line of credit to you based on the amount of your deposit. This can help you establish a credit history and improve your credit score over time.

Building and maintaining good credit takes time and effort, but it's worth it in the long run. By following these tips and being disciplined about your finances, you can improve your credit score and secure a brighter financial future for yourself.

Common mistakes to avoid when trying to improve your credit score

Here are a few common mistakes people make when trying to improve their credit scores:

- Closing old credit accounts. Many people think that closing old credit accounts will help improve their credit score, but this is not always the case. Closing old accounts can hurt your credit score because it reduces your overall credit limit, which can cause your credit utilization ratio to increase. Instead of closing old accounts, try to keep them open and active.
- Only making minimum payments on credit cards. Only making the minimum payment on your credit card can hurt your credit score because it can increase your credit utilization ratio. To avoid this, try to pay more than the minimum payment each month, and aim to pay off your credit card balances in full.
- Applying for too much credit at once. Each time you apply for a new credit card or loan, it can cause a small, temporary drop in your credit score. To avoid this, try to limit the number of new accounts you open, and don't apply for more credit than you need.
- Not checking your credit report regularly. Your credit report contains detailed information about your credit history, and it's a good idea to review it regularly to make sure everything is accurate. If you don't check your credit report, you may not be aware of errors that could be hurting your credit score. You can request a free copy of your credit report from each of the three major credit bureaus (Equifax, Experian, and TransUnion) once a year.

- Not disputing errors on your credit report. If you find any errors on your credit report, it's important to dispute them as soon as possible. Ignoring errors on your credit report can cause your credit score to be lower than it should be. You can dispute errors by contacting the credit bureau directly, or you can use a credit repair service to help you with the process.

By avoiding these mistakes and being disciplined about your finances, you can improve your credit score and secure a better financial future for yourself.

The role of credit utilization in your credit score

Credit utilization is the amount of credit that you are using relative to your credit limit. For example, if you have a credit card with a $1,000 limit and you have a balance of $500, your credit utilization would be 50%. Your credit utilization ratio is an important factor in determining your credit score, and it's generally best to keep your credit utilization ratio as low as possible. This is because a high credit utilization ratio can indicate to lenders that you are relying heavily on credit and may be at a higher risk of defaulting on your debts.

To improve your credit score, try to keep your credit utilization ratio below 30% on each of your credit cards. If you have multiple credit cards, spread your balances out evenly to avoid having one card maxed out. Ideally, work towards paying off your credit card balances in full each month to avoid having a high credit utilization ratio. By keeping your credit utilization ratio low, you can improve your credit score and show lenders that you are a responsible borrower. This can help you qualify for better interest rates and terms on future loans and credit cards.

Credit or debit cards?

Using a debit card or cash instead of a credit card can be a good way to control your spending if you have difficulty sticking to a budget. With a debit card, you can only spend the money that you have in your bank account, so you won't be able to overspend or accumulate credit card debt. However, it's important to note that using credit cards responsibly can help you improve your credit score, and having available credit can be beneficial in certain situations. For example, if you have an emergency expense and you need to pay for it with a credit card, it's helpful to have one available. Additionally, even if you pay off your credit card balances in full each month, having a credit card can help improve your credit score because it shows lenders that you are using credit responsibly.

Whether you use a credit card, debit card, or cash to manage your spending is a personal decision, and the right choice will depend on your individual circumstances and financial goals. It's important to consider the pros and cons of each option and choose the one that works best for you.

Using Debt Wisely

Credit and debt management are essential skills for achieving financial stability and success. By learning about the different types of credit and how to manage debt effectively, you have taken an important step towards achieving financial stability and success.

While debt can be a useful tool for financing large purchases or investing in income-generating assets, it is important to use it wisely. By developing healthy credit habits and minimizing unnecessary debt, you can avoid financial pitfalls and position yourself for long-term financial success.

Remember, credit and debt can be powerful tools when used wisely. By understanding how to use credit to your advantage and managing your debt effectively, you can increase your earning potential and build a strong financial foundation for the future.

Take control of your credit and debt, and use it wisely to help you achieve your financial goals. With careful planning and a commitment to responsible credit and debt management, you can live a financially secure life and achieve your financial dreams

.

Build a Diversified Income Stream

I had always been passionate about writing, but I had never considered it as a source of income. I had a good job as a financial analyst and I was comfortable, but I couldn't shake the feeling that I was meant for something more. I decided to take a chance and start writing on the side. I didn't know if it would turn into anything, but I figured it was worth a shot. I started by writing articles for local publications and sharing my work on social media.

To my surprise, people seemed to really enjoy my writing. I received positive feedback and even started getting paid for my articles. I was thrilled that I had found a way to share my passion with others and make a little extra money at the same time. As my writing career began to grow, I started to see the benefits of diversifying my income. Not only was I able to do something I loved, but I also had a backup source of income in case something happened to my day job.

I learned that it's important to have multiple streams of income and to never be afraid to try something new. With a little bit of hard work and determination, you can turn your passions into a viable career.

The importance of diversifying your income

Diversifying your income is an important aspect of financial planning because it can help reduce your financial risk, increase your earning potential, and provide a financial safety net. By spreading your sources of income across a variety of sources, you can help protect yourself against financial risks such as job loss or market downturns and increase your financial stability. Additionally, diversifying your income can help you increase your overall earning potential by taking advantage of multiple streams of income. This can help you build a more robust financial foundation and achieve long-term financial stability. Finally, diversifying your income can also help you build a financial safety net by providing a cushion in case of unexpected financial challenges. By diversifying your income, you can help ensure that you have a steady flow of income coming in from multiple sources, which can help you maintain your financial stability in the long term.

Different types of income sources

Diversifying your income is an important aspect of financial planning because it can help reduce your financial risk, increase your earning potential, and provide a financial safety net. There are many different sources of income that you can consider as part of your income diversification strategy, such as employment income, self-employment income, investment income, passive income, government benefits, pension income, and savings and emergency funds. The gig economy, or the trend towards temporary or flexible jobs, is also a potential source of income that can help you diversify your income. It's important to carefully consider which sources of income are right for you based on your financial goals and risk tolerance, and it may be helpful to work with a financial advisor to develop a diversified income strategy that aligns with your financial goals.

Strategies for building a diversified income stream

Taking on a second job is a strategy that you can consider as part of your efforts to build a diversified income stream. Some potential benefits of a second job include providing an additional source of income, an opportunity to learn new skills or gain new experiences, and potentially flexible work hours. However, it's important to carefully consider the time and energy required for a second job, as well as any potential impact on your other commitments and relationships. You should also carefully evaluate the potential financial benefits and consider any additional expenses that may come with a second job.

Working in the gig economy can be a way to diversify your income and potentially increase your earning potential, but it's important to carefully consider the potential advantages and disadvantages. Some potential benefits of gig work include flexibility, the ability to diversify your income, and the potential for higher income. However, gig work may also come with drawbacks such as a lack of job security, a lack of benefits, and tax implications. It's important to carefully consider these factors before deciding whether gig work is a good fit for you.

Consulting work can be a way to diversify your income stream by providing an additional source of income and potentially increasing your overall earning potential. Consulting work often involves providing expert advice or services to clients on a temporary or project-based basis, and it can be a good way to leverage your skills and expertise in a specific area. Some potential benefits of consulting work include flexibility, the potential for higher income, and the opportunity to use your expertise in a more focused and specialized way. However, consulting work may also come with drawbacks such as a lack of job security, a lack of benefits, and tax implications.

Renting out a room can be a way to diversify your income by providing an additional source of income. Some potential benefits of renting out a room include the additional source of income and the potential for passive income. However, there are also considerations to keep in mind when renting out a room, such as the impact on your privacy, legal and tax implications, and the need for maintenance and repairs.

Selling products or services online can be a way to diversify your income by providing an additional source of income. Some potential benefits of selling products or services online include the potential for passive income, low overhead costs, and a wide reach. However, there are also considerations to keep in mind when selling products or services online, such as competition, the need for marketing and advertising, and payment processing fees.

Maintaining flexibility and adaptability

It's important to be flexible and adaptable when looking at a diversified income stream because changes in market conditions, personal circumstances, and opportunities and challenges can impact the performance of different income sources. Being flexible and adaptable can help you to respond to these changes and adjust your income streams as needed in order to align with your personal circumstances and financial goals.

Diversified income that aligns with goals and interests

It's important to develop diversified income streams that align with your goals and interests because it can increase your motivation and enjoyment in your work, help to ensure that your income streams are aligned with your values, and increase your chances of long-term success.

It's important to abandon diversified income streams that are not performing well because maintaining underperforming income streams can divert resources and attention away from more lucrative opportunities, increase risk, and potentially misalign with financial goals. By regularly evaluating the performance of your income streams and adjusting as needed, you can ensure that your income streams are helping you to achieve your financial goals.

Case studies of successful diversified income streams

The following are some case study examples that might help inspire you with some ideas about how to build a diversified income stream:

Case study: Alice

Alice is a recent college graduate who is working as a data entry clerk to pay off her student loans. However, Alice is interested in a career in marketing and has always been fascinated by the way that companies use data to target their advertising. She finds her data entry work to be monotonous and unfulfilling, and she is not motivated to perform her work to the best of her abilities.

One potential fix for Alice's problem could be to develop an income stream that aligns more closely with her interests and goals. For example, she could consider taking on marketing internships or freelance projects that allow her to use her skills and interests in data analysis to create targeted advertising campaigns. She could also consider pursuing a marketing degree or certification to further develop her skills and increase her chances of success in the field. By developing an income stream that aligns more closely with her interests and goals, Alice may be more motivated and engaged in her work and more likely to achieve long-term success.

Case study: Bob

Bob is a software developer who has worked in the tech industry for several years. He is currently employed full-time at a software company, but he has always been interested in entrepreneurship and has been saving money to start his own business. Bob decides to take the plunge and launches a small software consulting business on the side, offering custom software development services to a range of clients.

Over time, Bob's consulting business grows and becomes a significant source of income for him. He can use the skills and experience he has gained in his full-time job to successfully serve his clients and grow his business. Bob continues to work full-time, but he can gradually reduce his hours as his consulting business becomes more successful. He is eventually able to transition working full-time on his own business and is able to achieve the financial independence and fulfillment he has always dreamed of.

In this example, Bob was able to successfully diversify his income stream by starting a small business on the side. By using the skills and experience he gained in his full-time job, he was able to build a successful consulting business that eventually became his primary source of income. By diversifying his income stream, Bob was able to achieve greater financial independence and fulfillment.

Common challenges and how to overcome them

Lack of time is a common challenge that individuals may face when building diversified sources of income. Building new income streams can be time-consuming, as it may involve researching potential income streams, networking with potential clients or partners, building and maintaining a business, and managing various tasks and responsibilities. This can be especially challenging if you are already working full-time or have other commitments, such as caring for a family or pursuing other hobbies or interests.

To overcome the challenge of lack of time when building diversified sources of income, it's important to prioritize your tasks and activities and focus on the most important ones first. This can help you to minimize distractions and ensure that you are using your time effectively. Time management techniques, such as creating a schedule or using a time-tracking tool, can also be helpful in managing your time and identifying areas where you can make improvements. Delegating tasks or responsibilities to others can also be an effective way to free up time and allow you to focus on building your income streams. For example, you might consider hiring an assistant or virtual assistant to handle some of your tasks or responsibilities, or you might delegate tasks to employees or team members. Automating tasks or processes can also help to free up time and allow you to focus on more important tasks. For example, you might consider using automation tools or software to handle tasks such as scheduling appointments, sending emails, or generating reports.

Managing your time effectively can be a key factor in building and maintaining diversified sources of income. By prioritizing tasks, using time management techniques, delegating tasks, and automating processes, you can find the time you need to build and maintain your income streams.

Lack of resources, such as money or equipment, can be a common challenge that individuals may face when building diversified sources of income. Building new income streams often requires financial resources, such as money to invest in a new business or equipment to get started. It can be challenging to find the financial resources needed to build a new income stream, especially if you are already stretched financially. To overcome the challenge of lack of resources when building diversified sources of income, it's important to be resourceful and creative. There may be low-cost or no-cost options for building a new income stream, such as starting a business that requires minimal upfront investment or leveraging free or low-cost tools and resources. You may also be able to seek out funding options, such as grants, loans, or investment from friends and family.

You may also have resources that you can use to get started, such as equipment, skills, or connections. It's important to carefully assess the resources you already have and consider how they can be leveraged to build a new income stream. Finally, you may be able to build your income stream slowly over time, investing resources as they become available and as your income stream grows. This can be a good option if you are unable to find the resources you need upfront or if you want to minimize risk.

It is important to be resourceful and creative when building diversified sources of income, and to consider all options for finding the resources you need to get started. By looking for low-cost or no-cost options, seeking out funding, using resources you already have, and building slowly, you may be able to overcome the challenge of lack of resources when building diversified sources of income.

Limited skills or experience can be a common challenge that individuals may face when building diversified sources of income. Building new income streams often requires specific skills or knowledge, and it can be challenging to build an income stream if you lack the necessary skills or experience. To overcome the challenge of limited skills or experience when building diversified sources of income, it's important to be proactive and open to learning. One way to do this is by learning new skills or acquiring new knowledge through education, training, or experience. Consider taking classes or workshops, earning a degree or certification, or gaining experience through internships or volunteer work. This can help you acquire the skills and knowledge you need to build your income stream.

Another strategy you can use is partnering with someone who has the skills or experience you need. This can be a good way to leverage the skills and knowledge of others while also building your own skills and experience. Finally, you may be able to outsource tasks or responsibilities to others who have the skills or experience you need. This can be a good way to focus on the tasks and responsibilities that you are most skilled at, while also taking advantage of the skills and experience of others.

It is important to be proactive and open to learning when building diversified sources of income. By learning new skills, partnering with someone who has the skills or experience you need, or outsourcing tasks, you may be able to overcome the challenge of limited skills or experience when building diversified sources of income.

Competition can be a common challenge that individuals may face when building diversified sources of income. Building new income streams often requires competing with others who may be offering similar products or services, and it can be challenging to build an income stream if you are competing with others who have more resources, experience, or a stronger reputation. To overcome the challenge of competition when building diversified sources of income, it's important to be proactive and strategic. One way to do this is by finding a niche market where there is less competition. This can involve targeting a specific segment of the market, offering a unique product or service, or focusing on a specific geographic area. By finding a niche market, you may be able to differentiate your products or services and to build a loyal customer base.

Another strategy you can use is building a strong brand to differentiate your products or services from competitors. This can involve creating a unique selling proposition, developing a strong visual identity, and building a positive reputation. By building a strong brand, you may be able to stand out from your competition and to attract more customers. Fostering strong relationships with customers can also be a key to building diversified sources of income. This can involve providing excellent customer service, being responsive to customer needs, and building trust. By building strong relationships with customers, you may be able to retain customers and to build a loyal customer base.

Finally, you can stay ahead of your competition by continuously improving your products or services. This can involve adding new features, improving the quality of your products or services, or increasing efficiency. By continuously improving your products or services, you may be able to stay ahead of your competition and to attract more customers. It is important to be proactive and strategic when building diversified sources of income. By finding a niche market, building a strong brand, fostering strong relationships with customers, and continuously improving your products or services, you may be able to overcome the challenge of competition when building diversified sources of income.

Next steps for creating a diversified income stream

In conclusion, building a diversified income stream is an important step in managing your personal finances. By having multiple sources of income, you can reduce your reliance on any one source and increase your financial stability. There are many ways to diversify your income, including earning passive income through investments, starting a side hustle, or seeking out new employment opportunities. It may take some effort to identify and pursue these opportunities, but the long-term benefits of a diversified income stream can be well worth it. Remember to continuously review and adjust your income streams to ensure that they are meeting your financial goals and needs.

Tax Planning and Preparation

A s I sat at my desk, surrounded by piles of paperwork and a mountain of tax forms, I couldn't help but feel a sense of déjà vu. It seemed like such a cliché - the exhausted accountant, falling asleep at their desk while trying to complete their taxes. But as I leaned back in my chair and closed my eyes, hoping to rest them for just a moment, I couldn't fight the overwhelming fatigue that had taken hold. Before I knew it, I was sound asleep. I must have dozed off for a good 20 minutes, because when I woke up, the room was pitch black and my computer screen was flickering.

As I sat there in a daze, trying to piece together what had just happened, it dawned on me that I had indeed fallen asleep while doing my taxes. I looked down and saw that my head was resting on a pile of documents, and there was a pen stuck to my cheek. It was a humbling moment, to say the least. But as I gathered up my things and headed to bed for the night, I couldn't help but feel grateful. I may have fallen asleep while doing my taxes, but at least I was able to get some much-needed rest in the process. And when it comes down to it, that's all that really matters. Even if it does seem like a bit of a cliché.

The purpose of the tax system

The tax system is a way for governments to collect revenue to fund public services and programs. Taxes are typically imposed on individuals and businesses based on their income, profits, and assets. The money collected from taxes is used to pay for a wide range of public goods and services, such as education, healthcare, infrastructure, and social welfare programs. The tax system is an important part of the government's fiscal policy, which determines how the government raises and spends money. The tax system can also be used as a tool to influence economic behavior and achieve policy goals, such as encouraging or discouraging certain types of consumption or investment.

In most countries, the tax system is administered by a government agency, such as the Internal Revenue Service (IRS) in the United States or the HM Revenue and Customs (HMRC) in the United Kingdom. These agencies are responsible for enforcing tax laws and collecting tax revenue. They may also provide guidance and assistance to taxpayers to help them understand their tax obligations and meet their tax filing and payment deadlines.

Who is required to pay taxes

In most countries, individuals and businesses are required to pay taxes on their income, profits, and assets. This means that you may be required to pay taxes on the money you earn from employment, self-employment, investments, and other sources. Depending on the type of income you receive, you may be required to pay different types of taxes, such as income tax, payroll tax, or capital gains tax. The amount of tax you owe depends on your income level and the tax rates that apply to your income. Tax rates can vary based on your income level, with higher earners generally paying a higher percentage of their income in taxes. Some countries have progressive tax systems, which means that higher earners pay a higher tax rate on their income. Other countries have flat tax systems, which means that everyone pays the same tax rate regardless of their income level.

In addition to income taxes, individuals and businesses may also be required to pay taxes on their profits, assets, and other financial transactions. For example, you may be required to pay property tax on your home or business, sales tax on purchases you make, or taxes on financial investments such as stocks or mutual funds. It's important to understand your tax obligations and pay your taxes on time to avoid penalties and interest charges. You may also be able to reduce your tax liability by claiming deductions or credits, such as the standard deduction or credits for charitable donations or education expenses.

How your tax liability is calculated

The amount of tax you owe depends on your income, the type of income you receive, and any deductions or credits you are eligible for. Your income tax liability is calculated based on the tax rates that apply to your income level and the tax laws in your country or jurisdiction. For example, if you earn a salary from employment, your employer will typically withhold a portion of your paychecks to cover your income tax liability. The amount of tax withheld will depend on the tax rates that apply to your income and any deductions or credits you are eligible for. You can use a tax calculator or consult with a tax professional to estimate your tax liability and determine how much you should have withheld from your paychecks. In addition to income taxes, you may also be required to pay taxes on other types of income, such as self-employment income, rental income, or investment income. The tax rates and rules that apply to these types of income may be different from those that apply to salary income.

You may be able to reduce your tax liability by claiming deductions or credits, such as the standard deduction, deductions for charitable donations or business expenses, or credits for education expenses or dependent care expenses. Deductions and credits can lower the amount of income that is subject to tax, reducing your overall tax bill. It's important to understand the deductions and credits that you are eligible for and claim them when you file your tax return.

Different types of tax systems

Tax rates can vary based on your income level, with higher earners generally paying a higher percentage of their income in taxes. This is known as a progressive tax system. In a progressive tax system, the tax rate increases as your income increases. For example, you may pay a lower tax rate on the first $50,000 of your income and a higher tax rate on income above $50,000. Progressive tax systems are designed to ensure that people with higher incomes pay a larger share of their income in taxes. The idea is that people with higher incomes can afford to pay a larger share of the cost of public goods and services, while those with lower incomes may struggle to pay the same percentage of their income in taxes.

Not all countries have progressive tax systems. Some countries have flat tax systems, in which everyone pays the same tax rate regardless of their income level. Flat tax systems are generally simpler and easier to administer than progressive tax systems, but they may be seen as less fair because they do not take into account differences in income.

It's important to understand the tax rates that apply to your income and how they may affect your tax bill. You may be able to reduce your tax liability by claiming deductions or credits, such as the standard deduction or credits for charitable donations or education expenses. It's also important to stay up to date with any changes to tax laws and rates, as these can affect your tax liability from one year to the next.

The importance of staying informed about tax law changes

Tax laws and rates can change from year to year, so it's important to stay informed about any updates that may affect your tax bill. Tax laws are typically enacted by governments as part of their fiscal policy, which determines how the government raises and spends money. Tax laws can be complex and may be subject to change as the government responds to economic conditions and policy priorities. Changes to tax laws can have a significant impact on your tax liability. For example, a change in tax rates or the introduction of new deductions or credits can affect the amount of tax you owe. It's important to stay up to date with these changes and understand how they may affect your tax situation.

There are several ways to stay informed about tax law changes. You can visit the website of the government agency responsible for administering taxes in your country or jurisdiction, such as the Internal Revenue Service (IRS) in the United States or the HM Revenue and Customs (HMRC) in the United Kingdom. You can also consult with a tax professional or use online tax resources to stay up to date on tax laws and changes. By staying informed about tax law changes, you can make sure you are paying the correct amount of tax and take advantage of any opportunities to reduce your tax liability. This can help you manage your finances more effectively and minimize any surprises when it comes time to file your tax return.

Reducing your tax liability with deductions and credits

You may be able to reduce your tax liability by claiming deductions or credits when you file your tax return. Deductions and credits are both ways to lower the amount of income that is subject to tax, which can reduce your overall tax bill. Deductions are expenses that you can subtract from your taxable income when you file your tax return. For example, you may be able to claim deductions for charitable donations, business expenses, or mortgage interest. Deductions can lower the amount of income that is subject to tax, which can reduce your tax liability. Credits are reductions in the amount of tax you owe. Credits are generally based on specific activities or expenses, such as education expenses, dependent care expenses, or energy-efficient home improvements. Credits are typically more valuable than deductions because they reduce your tax bill dollar for dollar.

It's important to understand the deductions and credits that you are eligible for and claim them when you file your tax return. This can help you reduce your tax liability and keep more of your hard-earned money. You can consult with a tax professional or use online tax resources to learn more about the deductions and credits that may be available to you.

The consequences of failing to pay taxes on time

Failing to pay your taxes on time can result in penalties and interest charges. It's important to stay up to date with your tax obligations and meet any deadlines for filing your tax return and paying your taxes. If you don't pay your taxes on time, you may be subject to late payment penalties and interest charges. The amount of the penalty and the interest rate will depend on the laws in your country or jurisdiction and the circumstances of your case. Late payment penalties and interest charges can add significantly to your tax bill and can be difficult to remove or waive once they are assessed.

To avoid penalties and interest charges, it's important to understand your tax obligations and meet any deadlines for filing your tax return and paying your taxes. If you are unable to pay your taxes in full, you may be able to arrange a payment plan with the tax agency to pay your taxes over time. You may also be able to request a hardship extension or other relief if you are unable to pay your taxes due to extenuating circumstances. By staying up to date with your tax obligations and paying your taxes on time, you can avoid costly penalties and interest charges and keep your finances on track.

The impact of taxes on financial planning

Paying taxes can affect your financial planning, as it reduces the amount of money you have available for other expenses or investments. However, the benefits of the public services and programs funded by taxes can also contribute to your overall financial well-being. Taxes are a necessary part of life, and they are used to fund a wide range of public goods and services that contribute to the overall well-being of society. These services and programs can include education, healthcare, infrastructure, and social welfare programs. By paying your fair share of taxes, you are helping to support these important public services and programs that can benefit you and your community.

At the same time, it's important to manage your tax burden and minimize your tax liability as much as possible. You can do this by staying informed about tax laws and claiming deductions and credits that you are eligible for. By reducing your tax burden, you can free up more of your income for other expenses or investments.

In summary, taxes are an important part of the financial landscape and can affect your financial planning. By staying informed about tax laws and minimizing your tax liability as much as possible, you can manage your finances effectively and take advantage of the benefits that public services and programs funded by taxes provide.

Know what deductions and credits you can claim

To maximize your deductions and reduce your tax burden, it's important to understand the deductions and credits that you are eligible for. There are many different deductions and credits that you may be able to claim on your tax return, depending on your circumstances and the laws in your country or jurisdiction. Some common deductions include charitable donations, business expenses, and mortgage interest. Credits can be based on a wide range of activities or expenses, such as education expenses, dependent care expenses, or energy-efficient home improvements.

To claim a deduction or credit, you must generally be able to prove that you are eligible for it. This usually requires documentation, such as receipts, invoices, or other proof of payment. It's important to keep good records of your deductions and credits so that you can claim them when you file your tax return. By understanding the deductions and credits that you are eligible for, you can make sure you are claiming all of the ones that you qualify for and reducing your tax burden as much as possible.

Keep good records

Proper record-keeping is essential for maximizing your deductions and credits and reducing your tax burden. To claim a deduction or credit, you generally need to be able to provide documentation to support your claim. This may include receipts, invoices, bank statements, or other records that show the amount of the deduction or credit and how it was incurred. It's important to keep good records of all of your deductions and credits, even if you are not sure whether you will be able to claim them on your tax return. By keeping accurate and complete records, you will be better prepared to claim deductions and credits when you file your tax return, and you will be more likely to be able to claim the full amount that you are eligible for.

To keep good records, you should consider keeping receipts, invoices, and other documentation in a safe and organized place. You may also want to use a spreadsheet or other record-keeping system to track your deductions and credits. By keeping good records, you can maximize your deductions and credits and reduce your tax burden. It's also important to keep your records in a safe and organized place, as you may need to provide them to the tax agency if you are audited.

Plan your deductions

To maximize your deductions and reduce your tax burden, you may want to consider timing your deductions to maximize their impact on your tax liability. This can involve considering when you incur certain expenses or make charitable donations, as well as when you file your tax return.

For example, if you have a high income in one year and a low income in another year, you may be able to claim deductions or credits in the high-income year to offset some of the tax you owe. This can be especially helpful if you are in a high tax bracket and would otherwise pay a large amount of tax on your high income. You may also be able to claim deductions or credits in the year that you incur certain expenses or make charitable donations, even if you do not file your tax return until the following year. This can allow you to claim deductions and credits earlier, which can help reduce your tax burden over time.

By considering the timing of your deductions and credits, you may be able to maximize their impact on your tax liability and reduce your tax burden. It's important to stay informed about tax laws and changes, and to consult with a tax professional if you have questions or need guidance.

Contribute to retirement accounts

Contributing to certain types of retirement accounts, such as 401(k)s or individual retirement accounts (IRAs), may be tax-deductible or qualify for a tax credit. This can be an effective way to reduce your tax burden and save for retirement at the same time.

For example, if you contribute to a 401(k) or traditional IRA, you may be able to claim a deduction for your contribution on your tax return. This can reduce the amount of income that is subject to tax, which can lower your tax bill. Alternatively, you may be able to claim a tax credit for contributions to certain types of retirement accounts, such as a Roth IRA. Tax credits are generally more valuable than deductions because they reduce your tax bill dollar for dollar.

It's important to understand the tax rules that apply to retirement accounts and to consult with a tax professional or financial advisor if you have questions. By contributing to retirement accounts and taking advantage of any tax benefits they offer, you can reduce your tax burden and save for the future at the same time.

Consider itemizing your deductions

If you have a lot of deductions, you may be better off itemizing your deductions rather than claiming the standard deduction. Itemizing your deductions allows you to claim specific deductions for certain expenses, such as charitable donations, mortgage interest, and business expenses. To itemize your deductions, you will need to complete a schedule of your deductions and attach it to your tax return.

Claiming the standard deduction is generally simpler and requires less documentation than itemizing your deductions. The standard deduction is a fixed amount that you can claim on your tax return without having to itemize your deductions. The amount of the standard deduction varies depending on your filing status and other factors. If you have a lot of deductions, you may be able to save more money on your taxes by itemizing your deductions rather than claiming the standard deduction. However, itemizing your deductions requires more work and documentation, and you may need to keep good records of your deductions to claim them on your tax return.

It's important to consider both options and determine which one will result in the lower tax bill. You can use a tax calculator or consult with a tax professional to estimate your tax liability under both scenarios and decide which one is right for you.

Consult with a tax professional

If you have complex financial circumstances or are unsure about how to claim deductions or credits, you may want to consider consulting with a tax professional. Tax professionals, such as certified public accountants (CPAs) or enrolled agents, have expertise in tax laws and can help you navigate the tax system and identify opportunities to reduce your tax burden. Tax professionals can provide a range of services, including preparing your tax return, reviewing your tax situation, and providing advice on tax planning and compliance. They can also help you understand your tax obligations and the deductions and credits that you are eligible for.

Working with a tax professional can be especially helpful if you have a complex tax situation, such as self-employment income, rental income, or investments. It can also be useful if you are facing a tax audit or other tax-related issues. By consulting with a tax professional, you can get expert advice on your tax situation and take advantage of opportunities to reduce your tax burden. It's important to choose a tax professional who is experienced and reputable, and to be honest and transparent about your tax situation to ensure that you get the best possible advice.

Gather your tax documents

To prepare and file your taxes efficiently, it's important to gather all the necessary tax documents before you start preparing your tax return. This includes documents such as W-2 forms, 1099 forms, and receipts for deductions and credits. W-2 forms are issued by your employer and report your wages and salaries, as well as the amount of tax withheld from your pay. You'll need to provide a copy of your W-2 form when you file your tax return. 1099 forms report various types of income, such as self-employment income, investment income, or rental income. You'll need to provide a copy of any 1099 forms you receive when you file your tax return.

Receipts and other documentation are generally required to claim deductions and credits on your tax return. Make sure you keep good records of any deductions and credits that you plan to claim, including receipts, invoices, and other documentation. By gathering all the necessary tax documents before you start preparing your tax return, you can ensure that you have all the information you need to file your taxes accurately and efficiently. It's also important to keep your tax documents in a safe and organized place, as you may need to provide them to the tax agency if you are audited.

Choose a filing method

To file your taxes efficiently, you'll need to choose a filing method. There are several options available, including electronic filing and paper filing. Electronic filing, also known as e-filing, is the process of submitting your tax return electronically using tax software or online services. E-filing is generally the easiest and quickest way to file your taxes, and it can also reduce the risk of errors on your tax return. Paper filing involves mailing a paper tax return to the appropriate tax agency. This is generally a slower process than e-filing and may be more prone to errors.

When choosing a filing method, you should consider factors such as your comfort level with technology, the complexity of your tax situation, and any deadlines for filing your tax return. By choosing the right filing method, you can file your taxes efficiently and ensure that your tax return is submitted accurately and on time. It's important to stay informed about tax laws and changes, and to consult with a tax professional if you have questions or need guidance.

Determine your filing status

To prepare and file your taxes efficiently, it's important to determine your filing status. Your filing status determines your tax rate and the amount of your standard deduction, which can affect the amount of tax you owe. In the United States, there are five main filing statuses: single, married filing jointly, married filing separately, head of household, and qualifying widow(er) with dependent child. Each filing status has its own set of rules and requirements, and you'll need to choose the one that applies to your situation. To determine your filing status, you'll need to consider factors such as your marital status, the number of dependents you have, and whether you are supporting a qualifying relative.

By determining your filing status correctly, you can ensure that you are paying the correct amount of tax and taking advantage of any deductions or credits that you are eligible for. It's important to stay informed about tax laws and changes, and to consult with a tax professional if you have questions or need guidance.

Calculate your taxable income

To prepare and file your taxes efficiently, you'll need to calculate your taxable income. Taxable income is the portion of your income that is subject to tax. To calculate your taxable income, you'll need to subtract deductions and credits from your total income. There are different types of deductions and credits that you may be eligible for, depending on your circumstances. Deductions reduce your taxable income by the amount of the deduction, while credits reduce your tax liability dollar for dollar.

To claim deductions and credits, you generally need to be able to prove that you are eligible for them. This usually requires documentation, such as receipts, invoices, or other proof of payment. It's important to keep good records of your deductions and credits so that you can claim them when you file your tax return. By calculating your taxable income accurately, you can ensure that you are paying the correct amount of tax. It's important to stay informed about tax laws and changes, and to consult with a tax professional if you have questions or need guidance.

Determine your tax liability

To prepare and file your taxes efficiently, you'll need to determine your tax liability. This involves using your taxable income and your tax rate to calculate the amount of tax you owe. Your tax rate is based on your taxable income and your filing status. Tax rates are typically progressive, which means that you pay a higher tax rate on higher levels of income.

To calculate your tax liability, you'll need to use a tax table or tax calculator to determine the amount of tax you owe based on your taxable income and tax rate. If you have already made tax payments throughout the year, such as through withholding from your pay, you can subtract these amounts to determine your net tax liability. By determining your tax liability accurately, you can ensure that you are paying the correct amount of tax. It's important to stay informed about tax laws and changes, and to consult with a tax professional if you have questions or need guidance.

File your tax return

To file your taxes efficiently, you'll need to file your tax return by the deadline. This generally involves submitting your tax return electronically or mailing a paper tax return to the appropriate tax agency.

If you are filing electronically, you'll need to use tax software or an online service to prepare and submit your tax return. You'll generally need to provide information about your income, deductions, and credits, as well as any required documentation. If you are filing a paper tax return, you'll need to complete the necessary forms and attach any required documentation, such as W-2 forms and 1099 forms. You'll then need to mail your tax return to the appropriate tax agency.

It's important to meet any deadlines for filing your tax return and paying your taxes. If you miss a deadline, you may be subject to penalties or interest. By filing your tax return on time, you can ensure that you are following tax laws and avoid any potential penalties or interest. It's important to stay informed about tax laws and changes, and to consult with a tax professional if you have questions or need guidance.

Managing Your Tax Situation Effectively

In conclusion, tax planning and preparation is an important aspect of managing your financial affairs. By understanding the tax system and the deductions and credits that you are eligible for, you can reduce your tax burden and keep more of your money. To prepare and file your taxes efficiently, you should gather all of the necessary tax documents, choose a filing method, determine your filing status, calculate your taxable income, determine your tax liability, and file your tax return by the deadline. You may also want to consider keeping good records, planning your deductions, contributing to retirement accounts, itemizing your deductions, and consulting with a tax professional to maximize your deductions and credits and minimize your tax burden. By following these steps and staying informed about tax laws and changes, you can effectively manage your tax situation and make the most of your financial resources.

Protecting Your Finances

As the COVID-19 pandemic rages on (even if in diminished form), it has become increasingly clear that many people's financial situations are far more precarious than they ever could have imagined. The economic disruption caused by the pandemic has resulted in widespread job loss and reduced income for countless individuals, leading to financial insecurity and uncertainty.

For those who previously enjoyed stable employment and financial stability, the pandemic has been a rude awakening. As businesses have closed or scaled back operations, layoffs and reduced hours have become all too common. Even those who have managed to hold onto their jobs have often seen their income and hours reduced.

In addition to these economic challenges, the pandemic has also resulted in increased expenses for many people. Unexpected medical bills related to COVID-19 and the need for additional household supplies and personal protective equipment have all added to the financial strain.

The pandemic has also had an impact on financial markets, leading to fluctuations in the value of investments and retirement savings. This has made it difficult for many individuals to plan for their financial future and has contributed to a sense of financial insecurity.

It's clear that the COVID-19 pandemic has made many people much more aware of the frailty of their financial situations. It has also highlighted the importance of financial planning and preparedness, as well as the value of having a plan for protecting your assets to weather any upcoming financial storm.

Understanding the types of insurance

There are many different types of insurance that can protect your assets. Here are a few examples of the types of insurance that are available:

- Health insurance: Health insurance helps cover the cost of medical care, such as doctor's visits, hospital stays, and prescription drugs. There are different types of health insurance policies, including group health insurance, individual health insurance, and employer-provided health insurance.

- Life insurance: Life insurance provides financial protection for your loved ones in the event of your death. There are different types of life insurance policies, including term life insurance, whole life insurance, and universal life insurance.
- Auto insurance: Auto insurance provides financial protection in the event of an accident involving your vehicle. Auto insurance policies generally cover damages to your vehicle, medical expenses, and liability for damages or injuries to other parties.
- Homeowners insurance: Homeowners insurance covers damages to your home and personal property, as well as liability for accidents that occur on your property. Homeowners insurance policies may also cover temporary living expenses if you are unable to live in your home due to damages.
- Liability insurance: Liability insurance covers damages or injuries that you may be responsible for, such as if you cause an accident or if someone is injured on your property. Liability insurance may be included in other types of insurance policies, such as auto insurance or homeowners' insurance, or it may be purchased as a standalone policy.

By understanding the different types of insurance that are available, you can determine which types of insurance you need to protect your assets.

Determining your insurance needs

To understand which types of insurance you need, you'll need to consider your specific circumstances and the assets you want to protect. This may involve evaluating your income, your savings, your debts, and your future financial goals. For example, if you have a family or dependents, you may want to consider life insurance to provide financial protection in the event of your death. If you own a home, you may want to consider homeowners insurance to protect your home and personal property from damages. If you have a car, you'll likely need to purchase auto insurance to cover damages or injuries that may occur in an accident.

It's also important to consider your liability risk. If you own a business, for example, you may want to consider liability insurance to protect against claims related to your business activities. If you have a high net worth, you may want to consider liability insurance to protect your assets from potential lawsuits. By evaluating your circumstances and the assets you want to protect, you can determine which types of insurance you need. It's important to review your insurance coverage periodically to make sure it still meets your needs as your circumstances change.

Shopping around for insurance

To understand insurance and how it protects your assets, it's important to understand the different types of insurance that are available, determine your insurance needs, and shop around for insurance. There are many different types of insurance, including health insurance, life insurance, auto insurance, homeowners' insurance, and liability insurance. Each type of insurance covers different risks and protects different types of assets. To understand which types of insurance you need, you'll need to consider your specific circumstances and the assets you want to protect. This may involve evaluating your income, your savings, your debts, and your future financial goals.

To find the right insurance policy at the best price, it's important to shop around and compare policies from different insurers. You can use online tools or consult with an insurance broker to help you find the right policy at the best price. It's important to consider not just the price of the policy, but also the coverage and exclusions, as these can affect your protection. In addition to shopping around, you may also be able to save on your insurance premiums by taking steps such as bundling multiple policies with the same insurer or increasing your deductible.

Reading and understanding your policy

To make sure your insurance coverage meets your needs and protects your assets, it's important to understand your insurance policy and know what is and is not covered. To do this, you should carefully read and understand your policy, paying attention to the coverage, exclusions and limitations, premiums and deductibles, and claims process. Your insurance policy should specify what types of risks and damages are covered by your policy. This may include damages to your home, your car, or your personal property, as well as medical expenses or liability for damages or injuries to others. However, it's important to be aware of any exclusions or limitations in your policy. These may exclude certain types of risks or damages from coverage or may limit the amount of coverage you have for certain risks.

Your insurance policy will also specify your premiums and deductibles. Your premiums are the amount you pay for your insurance coverage, while your deductible is the amount you need to pay out of pocket before your insurance coverage kicks in. It's important to understand how these work and how they may affect your coverage. In the event of a loss or accident, you'll need to follow the claims process specified in your policy. This may involve contacting your insurer, providing documentation, and following certain procedures. By understanding your insurance policy and the claims process, you can ensure that you are properly protected and know what to do in the event of a loss or accident. If you have any questions about your policy, don't hesitate to ask your insurer or an insurance professional for clarification.

Reviewing your insurance coverage periodically

To ensure that your insurance coverage continues to meet your needs and protect your assets, it's important to review your insurance coverage periodically. Your insurance needs may change over time, so it's important to keep your coverage up to date. When reviewing your insurance coverage, you should consider any changes in your circumstances, such as getting married, having a child, or buying a new home, as well as changes in the value of your assets, changes in insurance laws or regulations, and changes in your insurance needs.

If you have experienced any significant changes in your circumstances, you may need to update your insurance coverage to make sure it is still appropriate for your needs. For example, if you have a child, you may want to consider increasing your life insurance coverage to provide financial protection for your family. Similarly, if you have purchased a new home, you may want to update your homeowner's insurance to make sure you have enough coverage to protect your home and personal property. It's also important to stay informed about changes in insurance laws and regulations, as these can affect your coverage. For example, if there are changes to the types of risks that are covered by your policy, you may need to adjust your coverage to make sure you are protected.

Finally, as your circumstances change, your insurance needs may change as well. It's important to review your coverage periodically to make sure it still meets your needs. By staying informed and reviewing your insurance coverage regularly, you can ensure that you have the right coverage to protect your assets and meet your needs. If you have any questions about your coverage, don't hesitate to ask your insurer or an insurance professional for guidance.

Creating an estate plan to protect your assets and plan for the future

When creating an estate plan to protect your assets and plan for the future, it's important to determine your goals and objectives. Consider your long-term financial goals and how you want to achieve them. Some common goals for estate planning include protecting your assets, planning for your own future care, and reducing taxes.

To protect your assets, you may want to create an estate plan that ensures your assets are distributed according to your wishes. If you become incapacitated or unable to make financial or medical decisions for yourself, an estate plan can help ensure that your care is managed according to your wishes. Estate planning can also help you minimize taxes on your estate and maximize the value of your assets for your loved ones.

By considering your goals and objectives, you can create an estate plan that meets your needs and helps you achieve your long-term financial goals. To do this, you'll need to gather your financial and legal documents, identify your assets, choose an estate planning attorney, decide on the best estate planning tools for your needs, and review and update your estate plan regularly.

Gather financial and legal documents

To create an effective estate plan, you'll need to gather all of your financial and legal documents. This may include wills, trust documents, deeds, insurance policies, investment accounts, and financial statements.

A will is a legal document that specifies how you want your assets to be distributed after your death. It may also appoint a guardian for any minor children. Trust documents outline the terms of a trust, which is a legal arrangement that allows you to hold assets for the benefit of yourself or others. Deeds are legal documents that transfer ownership of real estate, so if you own real estate, you'll need to include deeds in your estate plan.

Insurance policies can provide financial protection for your loved ones in the event of your death or disability. Make sure to include copies of your insurance policies in your estate plan. Investment accounts, such as 401(k)s or IRAs, should also be included in your estate plan. Make sure to include any account numbers and beneficiary designations. Financial statements, such as bank statements and credit card statements, can help you get a complete picture of your financial situation. Make sure to include copies of your financial statements in your estate plan.

Identify your assets

To create an effective estate plan, it's important to identify all of your assets. This includes real estate, such as a home or rental property, as well as investment accounts, like 401(k)s or IRAs. You should also consider your personal property, such as jewelry, art, and collectibles, as well as any businesses, patents, or other intellectual property. Make a list of all your assets and consider their value and importance. By identifying all your assets, you can create an estate plan that covers all your assets and ensures they are protected according to your wishes. Make sure to include any deeds, mortgage documents, account numbers, and beneficiary designations as you create your estate plan.

Choose an estate planning attorney

To create an estate plan that meets your needs and complies with state and federal laws, it's important to choose an estate planning attorney. An estate planning attorney is a legal professional who specializes in creating estate plans that meet the needs and goals of their clients. When choosing an estate planning attorney, look for someone who has experience in estate planning and is familiar with the laws in your state. You should also look for an attorney who is responsive and easy to communicate with, as you'll be working closely with them to create your estate plan. Don't be afraid to shop around and get quotes from multiple attorneys. It's important to find an attorney who is a good fit for your needs and budget.

Decide on the best estate planning tools

When creating an estate plan, you'll need to decide on the best tools for your needs. There are several options available, including wills, trusts, powers of attorney, and advance healthcare directives. A will is a legal document that specifies how you want your assets to be distributed after your death. It may also appoint a guardian for any minor children. A trust is a legal arrangement that allows you to hold assets for the benefit of yourself or others, and can be used to protect assets, minimize taxes, or plan for future care. A power of attorney allows you to designate someone to make financial or medical decisions on your behalf if you become incapacitated, while an advance healthcare directive is a legal document that specifies your wishes for medical treatment in the event that you are unable to make decisions for yourself. Your attorney can help you determine which tools are best for your needs and explain how each tool works and how it can be used to meet your goals.

Review and update your estate plan regularly

It's important to review and update your estate plan regularly to ensure that it meets your needs and complies with state and federal laws. There are several reasons why you may need to update your estate plan. For example, if you experience significant life changes, such as getting married, having children, or getting divorced, you'll need to update your estate plan to reflect these changes. Additionally, estate planning laws can change over time, so it's important to make sure that your estate plan is up to date and compliant with current laws. If your financial situation changes significantly, you may also need to update your estate plan to reflect these changes. For example, if you acquire new assets or incur significant debts, you'll need to update your estate plan to reflect these changes. It's a good idea to review your estate plan every few years or whenever you experience a major life change. By reviewing and updating your estate plan regularly, you can ensure that it continues to meet your needs and protect your assets.

Protecting yourself against financial fraud and scams

Phishing scams are a common type of financial fraud that involves attempting to obtain sensitive information, such as passwords or bank account numbers, by pretending to be a legitimate organization or individual. Phishers often use fake websites or emails to trick victims into revealing their personal information. They may pretend to be a bank or other financial institution, a government agency, or even a friend or family member. They may use urgent or threatening language to try to get the victim to act quickly, or they may use a sense of urgency or fear to try to get the victim to comply.

To protect yourself against phishing scams, it's important to be cautious of emails or calls from unknown sources, especially if they ask for personal information or money. Don't click on links or download attachments from unknown sources, and don't give out personal information, such as your social security number or bank account numbers, to strangers or unsolicited calls or emails. If you receive an email or call that seems suspicious, verify the identity of the sender before responding or providing any information. It's also a good idea to use strong and unique passwords for all of your accounts and to use security software, such as antivirus and firewall protection, to protect your computer and personal information.

Investment scams

Investment scams are a common type of financial fraud that involves promising high returns on investments, but in reality, the investment is a fraud and the victim loses their money. Investment scams can take many forms, such as Ponzi schemes, pyramid schemes, or fake investment opportunities. Fake investment opportunities may involve promising high returns on investments in things like real estate, precious metals, or other assets, but in reality, the investment is a fraud and the victim loses their money.

To protect yourself against investment scams, it's important to be cautious of any investment opportunity that seems too good to be true. Do your research and verify the legitimacy of the investment before putting any money into it. Be wary of high-pressure sales tactics or promises of guaranteed returns, and don't invest money that you can't afford to lose. It's also a good idea to diversify your investments and work with a financial advisor you trust.

Ponzi or pyramid schemes

A Ponzi or pyramid scheme is a type of financial fraud that involves using money from new investors to pay returns to earlier investors, with the scammer keeping a portion of the money for themselves. Eventually, the scheme collapses, and the investors lose their money. In a Ponzi scheme, the scammer typically promises high returns on investments and may use fake documents or testimonials to convince potential investors to hand over their money. However, the investment is actually a fraud, and the money is not being used for legitimate investment purposes. Instead, the scammer uses the money from new investors to pay returns to earlier investors, creating the appearance of a successful investment. The scheme collapses when the scammer can no longer attract new investors or when the returns promised to earlier investors become unsustainable.

A pyramid scheme works in a similar way, but the focus is on recruiting new members rather than investing money. Participants in a pyramid scheme are usually required to pay a fee to join and are promised a share of the money generated by recruiting additional members. However, the scheme collapses when it becomes difficult to recruit new members and the returns promised to earlier participants become unsustainable.

To protect yourself against Ponzi or pyramid schemes, it's important to be cautious of any investment opportunity that seems too good to be true. Do your research and verify the legitimacy of the investment before putting any money into it. Be wary of high-pressure sales tactics or promises of guaranteed returns, and don't invest money that you can't afford to lose.

Lottery scams

Lottery scams are a common type of financial fraud that involve falsely claiming that the victim has won a lottery or sweepstakes and asking for personal information or money to claim the prize. Scammers may use fake emails, texts, or phone calls to tell the victim that they have won a large sum of money or a valuable prize, such as a car or a vacation. The scammer may ask the victim to pay a fee to claim the prize or may ask for personal information, such as their bank account number or social security number, in order to "process the prize."

However, in reality, the victim has not won anything, and the scammer is using the opportunity to steal the victim's money or personal information. Lottery scams can be difficult to detect, as scammers may use official-looking logos or websites to make the scam seem legitimate.

To protect yourself against lottery scams, it's important to remember that you can't win a lottery or sweepstakes that you didn't enter. If you receive an email, text, or phone call claiming that you have won a prize, be suspicious and do not respond to the message or provide any personal information. It's also a good idea to be cautious of any emails or calls from unknown sources, especially if they ask for money or personal information. If you believe that you may have been the victim of a lottery scam, report it to the authorities or to a trusted organization, such as the Federal Trade Commission.

Charity scams

Charity scams are a common type of financial fraud that involve pretending to be a legitimate charity and soliciting donations, but in reality, the money goes to the scammer and not the charity. Charity scams can take many forms, such as fake charities, fraudulent fundraising campaigns, or charity fraud schemes.

Fake charities are organizations that pretend to be legitimate charities but are actually scams. They may use fake websites or social media pages to solicit donations, or they may use telemarketing or door-to-door fundraising to collect money. In reality, the money goes to the scammer and not to any charitable cause.

Fraudulent fundraising campaigns are fundraising campaigns that use fake charities or fake causes to solicit donations. They may use social media or other online platforms to spread false information or emotional appeals in order to solicit donations.

Charity fraud schemes are schemes in which scammers use fake charities or fraudulent fundraising campaigns to steal money or personal information from donors. They may use fake websites or social media pages to solicit donations or may use telemarketing or door-to-door fundraising to collect money.

To protect yourself against charity scams, it's important to be cautious of any charity that you are not familiar with. Do your research and verify the legitimacy of the charity before donating money. Be wary of high-pressure sales tactics or emotional appeals, and don't give out personal information, such as your bank account number or social security number, to strangers or unsolicited calls or emails.

Employment scams

Employment scams are a common type of financial fraud that involve offering fake job opportunities and requiring the victim to pay upfront fees or provide personal information. Employment scams may use fake job listings or fake job placement agencies to lure victims into applying for non-existent jobs. They may also use fake websites or emails to solicit applications for fake jobs.

Once the victim has applied for the job, the scammer may ask for upfront fees to cover the cost of training or other expenses, or they may ask for personal information, such as a social security number or bank account number. In reality, the job does not exist, and the scammer is using the opportunity to steal the victim's money or personal information.

To protect yourself against employment scams, it's important to be cautious of any job opportunity that seems too good to be true or that requires upfront fees or personal information. Do your research and verify the legitimacy of the job and the company before applying or providing any personal information. Be wary of high-pressure sales tactics or promises of guaranteed employment, and don't pay any money to anyone in exchange for a job.

Debt relief scams

Debt relief scams are a common type of financial fraud that involve promising to help consumers pay off their debts for a fee, but in reality, the scammer takes the victim's money and does not provide any debt relief. Debt relief scams may use fake websites or telemarketing to solicit consumers who are struggling with debt. The scammer may promise to negotiate with creditors to reduce the victim's debt or to provide a loan to help pay off the debt. However, the scammer does not provide any debt relief and may take the victim's money without providing any services. Debt relief scams can be difficult to detect, as scammers may use official-looking logos or websites to make the scam seem legitimate.

To protect yourself against debt relief scams, it's important to be cautious of any company that promises to help you pay off your debts for a fee. Do your research and verify the legitimacy of the company before agreeing to any services or paying any money. Be wary of high-pressure sales tactics or promises of guaranteed debt relief, and don't provide any personal information, such as your social security number or bank account number, to strangers or unsolicited calls or emails. If you are struggling with debt and need help, consider working with a trusted financial advisor or credit counseling service.

Identity theft

Identity theft is a type of financial fraud that involves using someone else's personal information, such as their name, address, or social security number, to commit financial crimes or to obtain credit, loans, or other benefits. Identity thieves may obtain personal information through a variety of methods, such as stealing mail or wallets, dumpster diving, or phishing scams.

Once the identity thief has obtained the personal information, they may use it to open credit card accounts, take out loans, or make purchases in the victim's name. This can result in significant financial losses for the victim and can damage their credit score.

To protect yourself against identity theft, it's important to be careful with your personal information and to safeguard it from unauthorized access. This includes shredding sensitive documents, using strong and unique passwords, and being cautious of phishing scams or other online threats. It's also a good idea to monitor your credit reports and financial accounts regularly to detect any unauthorized activity. If you believe that you may be the victim of identity theft, it's important to report it to the authorities and to take steps to secure your personal information and restore your credit.

Safeguarding your finances and assets

In conclusion, it is important to take steps to protect your finances and assets from financial frauds and scams, as well as to plan for the future and ensure that your assets are protected in case of unexpected events. This includes being aware of the most common types of financial frauds, such as investment scams, lottery scams, charity scams, employment scams, debt relief scams, identity theft, and phishing scams, and taking precautions to protect yourself and your financial well-being.

In addition to protecting yourself against financial frauds, it's also important to consider insurance as a way to protect your assets and plan for the future. Insurance can provide financial protection in case of unexpected events, such as accidents, illnesses, or natural disasters, and can help to minimize the financial impact of these events on you and your loved ones.

Estate planning is another important aspect of financial planning and protection. Estate planning involves organizing and managing your assets in a way that ensures that your wishes are carried out after your death and that your assets are distributed according to your wishes. This can include creating a will or trust, designating beneficiaries, and making arrangements for the care of minor children or dependents.

Final Thoughts

Personal finance is an important aspect of our daily lives and has a significant impact on our financial well-being and security. By understanding the basics of personal finance and learning how to manage our money and assets effectively, we can make informed decisions about our financial future and work towards our financial goals.

In this book, we have explored various topics related to personal finance, including budgeting, saving, investing, tax planning and preparation, insurance, estate planning, and financial fraud protection. By learning about these topics, you have gained valuable knowledge and skills that will help you to take control of your finances and make informed decisions about your financial future.

As you continue to learn and grow your personal finance knowledge, it's important to stay up-to-date with changes in financial laws and regulations, as well as to seek the advice of trusted financial professionals when needed. By taking a proactive approach to your personal finance, you can work towards financial stability and security, and achieve your financial goals. Be careful with your financial decision and live a happy and prosperous life!

BIBLIOGRAPHY

Carlson, Benjamin P. 2020. *Don't Fall for It: A Short History of Financial Scams*. Hoboken New Jersey: John Wiley & Sons.

Griffin, Michael P., 2017. Personal Financial Planning: Guide to Setting Goals, Protecting Assets, Investing and Gaining Security for a Good Life, BarCharts, Inc, Newburyport.

Hill, Napoleon., 2011. *Think and grow rich*. Hachette UK.

Housel, Morgan. 2020. *The Psychology of Money: Timeless Lessons on Wealth Greed and Happiness*. Hampshire Great Britain: Harriman House.

Kallen, Stuart A. 2021. *Managing Credit and Debt*. San Diego CA: ReferencePoint Press.

Kobliner, Beth. 2017. *Get a Financial Life: Personal Finance in Your Twenties and Thirties*. New York: Touchstone.

Saul-Sehy, Joe and Guy-Birken, Emily. 2021. *Stacked: Your Super-Serious Guide to Modern Money Management*. New York: Avery an imprint of Penguin Random House.

Torabi, Farnoosh. 2011. *The Young Professional's Guide to Taking Control of Your Money*. Upper Saddle River N.J: FTPress.

Virani Shazia. 2021. *Savvy Real Estate Investing Create a Passive Income Stream and Make Money in Your Sleep*. Vancouver: Self-Counsel Press.

Welch Stewart H and J. Winston Busby. 2019. J.k. *Lasser's New Rules for Estate Retirement and Tax Planning: Keep More Today Leave More to Your Heirs Tomorrow*. Sixth ed. Hoboken NJ: John Wiley & Sons.

Wright Scott. 2019. *Money Management: The Ultimate Guide to Budgeting Frugal Living Getting Out of Debt Credit Repair and Managing Your Personal Finances in a Stress-Free Way*. Place of publication not identified: Bravex Publications.

ABOUT THE AUTHOR

Christopher Truman began his career as a corporate financial analyst in Oakland, California for one of the nation's largest savings and loans. Christopher received his undergraduate and master's degrees in Economics from universities in California and Texas, respectively.

After several years of working in California, Christopher moved to Bryan, Texas where he took on a new role as a senior financial analyst at a super-regional bank. In this position, Christopher was responsible for analyzing financial data and providing insights and recommendations to senior management.

In his free time, Christopher enjoys spending time with his family, which includes his wife, two children, and their dog and horse. When he's not working, Christopher can be found running or hiking in the countryside. Christopher is excited to share his knowledge and expertise with readers through his new book, "Are You Making the Most of Your Money? A Personal Guide for Achieving Financial Success."

www.ingramcontent.com/pod-product-compliance
Lightning Source LLC
Chambersburg PA
CBHW070942210326
41520CB00021B/7011